C000110009

Songs of Our Hearts, Meditations of Our Souls

# Songs of Our Hearts, Meditations of Our Souls

## PRAYERS FOR BLACK CATHOLICS

Edited by Cecilia A. Moore, PH.D., C. Vanessa White, D.MIN.,
and Paul M. Marshall, S.M.

ST. ANTHONY MESSENGER PRESS

Cincinnati, Ohio

## RESCRIPT

In accord with the *Code of Canon Law*, I hereby grant my permission to publish *Songs of Our Hearts, Meditations of Our Souls: Prayers for Black Catholics*, edited by Cecilia A. Moore, PH.D., C. Vanessa White, D.MIN., and Paul M. Marshall, S.M.

Most Reverend Carl K. Moeddel
Vicar General and Auxiliary Bishop
of the Archdiocese of Cincinnati
Cincinnati, Ohio
October 16, 2006

The permission to publish is a declaration that a book or pamphlet is considered to be free from doctrinal or moral error. It is not implied that those who have granted the permission to publish agree with the contents, opinions or statements expressed.

Scripture passages have been taken from *New American Bible With Revised New Testament and Revised Psalms*, copyright ©1991, 1986, 1970 by the Confraternity of Christian Doctrine (CCD), Washington, D.C., and are used with permission. All rights reserved. No part of the *New American Bible* may be reproduced in any form without permission in writing from the copyright owner.

Cover design by Constance Wolfer.
Cover illustration is a quilt, "Christ Bearing the Cross," sewn by Michael Cummings, 2003.
Book design by Phillips Robinette, O.F.M.

LIBRARY OF CONGRESS CATALOGING-IN-PUBLICATION DATA

Songs of our hearts, meditations of our souls : prayers for Black Catholics / edited by Cecilia A. Moore, C. Vanessa White, and Paul M. Marshall.
    p. cm.
  ISBN-13: 978-0-86716-694-1 (pbk. : alk. paper)
  ISBN-10: 0-86716-694-0 (pbk. : alk. paper)  1. Catholic Church—Prayer-books and devotions—English. 2. African American Catholics—Prayer-books and devotions—English. I. Moore, Cecilia Annette. II. White, C. Vanessa. III. Marshall, Paul M.

BX2110.S72 2006
242'.80208996073—dc22

                          2006033376


ISBN 978-0-86716-694-1

Copyright ©2006, Cecilia A. Moore, PH.D., C. Vanessa White, D.MIN., and Paul M. Marshall, S.M. All rights reserved.

Published by St. Anthony Messenger Press
28 W. Liberty St.
Cincinnati, OH 45202
www.AmericanCatholic.org

Printed in the United States of America.
Printed on acid-free paper.

08 09 10 5 4 3 2

# Dedication

The editors wish to thank all who contributed prayers for this book. Your generosity in sharing your prayers is a gift to the entire community. We also thank St. Anthony Messenger Press for investing in books designed by and for the Black Catholic community. In particular, we thank Lisa Biedenbach and Ericka McIntyre for their tremendous dedication to the project. And, most of all, we thank our ancestors whose faith and prayer inspired us as we completed this book. It is to our ancestors in the faith that we dedicate our work.

# Contents

## PART TWO: *"THIS LITTLE LIGHT OF MINE"*
## PRAYERS FOR CHILDREN AND FAMILIES  /  15

# Introduction to
# African American Spirituality

*There's a sweet, sweet spirit in this place,*
*And I know that it's the Spirit of the Lord.*
*There are sweet expressions on each face,*
*And I know they feel the presence of the Lord.*[1]

Sister Thea Bowman, an African American religious, would often be asked to lead prayer at the annual meeting of Black clergy and religious women and men. Many times she began with a song about the sweet Spirit who gave life to her and to all human persons. At one such gathering, a priest remarked at the conclusion of her prayer, "She is surely a praying woman."

The words above cannot contain the real content of Sister Thea's prayer. When she prayed, you felt it. When she sang about the sweetness of the Spirit, you sensed that it was real as the peace of the Spirit that descended upon you, the listener.

We begin our reflections in *Songs of Our Hearts, Meditations of Our Souls* with this reference to Sister Thea because she embodied the

Spirit's presence, so central for any presentation about prayer in the African American tradition. She once spoke about prayer and spirituality in this way:

> Spirituality is conscious contact with the Spirit that is God, who is above us, who transcends and inspires us. It is conscious contact with the spirit that is "self," with the inner-self where memory, imagination, intellect, feelings and body are caught up in the search for humanity.[2]

The words of her song address elements that characterize prayer in the African American tradition. Prayer is an experience of God. A person in prayer connects with the deepest dimension of her being. There, in the experience, a person transcends the circumstances of her life. Joy, peace, fulfillment, assurance—these terms are often used to convey the effects of prayer within a person. Sister Thea named the experience "sweet." It is our hope that readers of this book will experience the sweetness of God that these prayers convey.

All religious practice includes various kinds and styles of prayer. In *Songs of Our Hearts, Meditations of Our Souls,* you will find liturgical prayer, prayers for families and communities, meditations, prayers of healing, prayers of inspiration, prayers of consolation, prayers of freedom and prayers of reconciliation. Fundamentally, prayer expresses the reach of the human spirit for what is beyond ordinary human experience. We have called this reach the spiritual dimension of life. Some may call it the height of human experience; others call it the depth of human experience. Expressions of prayer provide a person with the ways and means to be soulful. *Soul* is often used to describe prayer expressions of African Americans. We believe that the readers of these prayers will experience a stirring within their spirits because of the human character and experiences related in the prayers.

The spiritual side of life when accessed gives purpose and meaning to the physical and mental aspects of life. The spiritual goes beyond just the way we think or use our bodies or express our emotions. The spiritual is the core of a person that shapes all of life's experiences. Authentic prayer emerges from the interior of a person, and the transformative power of prayer takes root within the soul and grows or influences one's being. It is at this level that prayer takes on a human perspective that easily transfers to others. Authentic prayer may start with an individual's experience, and it is real. This reality invites others to contemplate their experience and connect or relate to the expression of prayer. Although prayer is born in subjectivity, it becomes the objective truth once expressed for others. This is the power of prayer. Prayer changes things and persons.

Traditions come together in this book of prayer and frame the content of *Songs of Our Hearts, Meditations of Our Souls*: the African American faith tradition, the Roman Catholic Christian Tradition and the variety of forms of prayer from African peoples. Some people may be surprised by this; others say it is about time that this has happened. Without being exhaustive in these introductory pages, we wish to speak about these traditions and what might help the reader/pray-er appreciate the chosen content.

## THE AFRICAN AMERICAN FAITH TRADITION

*"It's me. It's me, O Lord, standing in the need of prayer...Not my mother, nor my father, but it's me, O Lord, standing in the need of prayer."*[3] In most hymnals of Black songs, one would find this spiritual. In the African American faith experience the desire for transformation is central. This transformation is understood as the spiritual experience that liberates a person. Freedom within and freedom in the world begins with God, the Spirit, taking charge within a person.

To begin to appreciate the African American faith tradition, we need to understand something of the development of African

Americans. Enslaved Africans brought to America as a labor force established a new spiritual tradition that has roots in the Christianity of the New World and also in the tribal traditions of the Africans. In this short space, however, the history of African peoples in the Americas cannot adequately be retold, but we can outline some characteristics that shape the African American faith experience.

The history of Africans in the Americas recounts sad stories of oppression, dehumanization and destruction of their human existence. Often we have wondered how African slaves affirmed themselves in the midst of oppression. Yet, somehow they did. A record of their achievement of affirming humanity is contained in the heritage of the spirituals and prayers which have been preserved. In many prayers within *Songs of Our Hearts, Meditations of Our Souls* you will find references to the spirituals. They were composed by peoples who were alien in America. In the contemporary world the framework of these hymns still provides a way for people who experience racism to express themselves. Although the world around African slaves said that they were not human or as equal a human person as whites,[4] the slaves claimed to be children of God worthy of God's care and love. From their African heritage they understood that they were spiritual beings connected, in body and spirit, with God and their ancestors. They expressed this connection in the songs and prayers about their life experience, or the dreams they had for a better future and the hope for a change of their conditions. There is a power, transformative power, in the spirituals and prayers of the enslaved. The African American theologian Howard Thurman, speaking of a renewed interest in the spirituals in the 1960s, agrees with this.

Despite the primary secular and political character of the movement [the Civil Rights movement] it found sources of inspiration and courage in the spiritual insights that had provided a windbreak for our forefathers against the brutalities of slavery and the establishing of a ground of hope undimmed by the contradictions which held them in tight embrace.[5]

Black spirituality's aim is liberation. Carlyle Fielding Stewart writing about Black spirituality agrees with Thurman. He declares that the "central components of this African American paradigm of freedom" explain "how this unique model of spirituality has created the substance and framework of human existence that has aided the soul survival of black people in America."[6]

Freedom is the consequence of Black spirituality. Many have written that Black spirituality and Black culture have created alternative modes of consciousness and existence that have sublimated the anger and dross of racism and oppression. The term *soul* is often used to describe the resulting positive culture. African American spirituality is the seedbed of the quest for human freedom. This model of human freedom differs from all others. Its very essence and nature has enabled African American people to face, confront and transcend spiritually their social and political condition. You will find social and political circumstances described in these prayers, and you will discover the expression of liberation that allows people to know their worth and move beyond the restrictions of their conditions.

Reconciliation is another grace of African American prayer. Beyond surviving the issue of growing and flourishing as a human community, the uplifting of the race has always been a central concern for the African American community. Prayer provided the perspective needed not to return hate for the hatred experienced. The theme about a great day of rejoicing when all of God's children would be together can be found in many prayers in *Songs of Our Hearts, Meditations of Our Souls*. Indeed, the liberating grace experienced is the light that shines to bring about the community/family desired by God.

The "assurance of grace" is a term used by Frank Thomas to describe the response of Black people to African American preachers.[7] Thomas asserts that the assurance of grace sustained, encouraged and liberated African American people. What he briefly describes in his book has been substantially described in Alfred Smith's presentation on the "Dynamics of Black Religion."

According to Smith, there are three ritual transformations that take place in the Black religious experience. The first is the process focused on the dynamics of transformation, or attending to the spirit or spirits with which one is in communion. Often, when a person observes someone praying, the pray-er seems to be in a different space as the prayer is offered. That space is often thought of as being "in the spirit." There is an enthusiasm and spontaneity in the prayer experience. A person may even seem to be in a trance or engaged in an ecstatic performance. This is a way of coping. It is a therapeutic experience for the person and for the community gathered in prayer. Within the transformative dynamic, natural images are used to conjure the mystical. Prayer styles are multiple during this conjuring act for freedom. What is understood in the experience is that the leader's experience and expression affects the entire community. The leader is a corporate shaman bringing healing to the community's human experience. The shaman's ecstatic performance brings liberation to everyone. Many of the prayers in *Songs of Our Hearts, Meditations of Our Souls* should be understood in this light. When using the prayers, you must keep in mind the community of believers with whom you pray and with whom you spiritually exist.

The second ritual dynamic is the spiritual-aesthetic dynamic in Black culture. Most often prayers are recited, but it seems like the person offering the prayer is singing. There are indeed patterns often used by the one leading prayer: style-switching, call and response, and improvisation. Ritually a double consciousness—the human and the spiritual—is lived out. Freedom occurs through the ecstasy performed.

Lastly, the power of this liberating prayer affects the political dynamics in Black culture. Within the prayers presented here, you will find references to the Exodus story of God freeing his people from Egypt. This paradigm provides meaning and purpose to the role Black religion and faith plays in this world. The focus is the community freed from oppression here and now. Changing the sociopolitical landscape is a promise of God and the work of God. Biblical heroes Moses and Jesus have brought about this new reality in the past, and now, the same power that motivated them energizes contemporary prophets to work for the betterment of society.

The journey to freedom is not only an interior experience, it is the freedom of a just society in which everyone counts and everyone participates. In these prayers, you will discover the expression, expectation and desire for a just, human, open, welcoming and inclusive society. Prayer and faith in the African American tradition are vibrant connections with a God who liberates.

Paul M. Marshall, S.M.

## NOTES

[1] *Lead Me, Guide Me: The African American Catholic Hymnal* (Chicago: G.I.A. Publications, Inc., 1987), number 75.

[2] Celestine Cepress, F.S.P.A., PH.D., ed., *Sister Thea Bowman, Shooting Star: Selected Writings and Speeches* (Winona, Minn.: Saint Mary's Press, Christian Brothers Publications, 1993), p. 38.

[3] *Lead Me, Guide Me*, number 216.

[4] Laws existed in the United States that claimed that slaves who were sixty percent human mimicked the full humanity which whites possessed but did not possess it.

[5] Howard Thurman, *Deep River and The Negro Spiritual Speaks of Life and Death* (Richmond, Ind.: Friends United Press, 1975), p. 3.

[6] Carlyle Fielding Stewart, III, *Soul Survivors: An African American Spirituality* (Louisville, Ky.: Westminster John Knox Press, 1997), p. 6.

[7] Frank A. Thomas, *They Like to Never Quit Praisin' God: The Role of Celebration in Preaching* (Cleveland: United Church Press, 1997), p. 3.

# Introduction to Prayer in the African American Catholic Tradition: When the Praises Go Up

*Praise Him, Praise Him*
*Praise Him in the Morning*
*Praise Him in the Noontime*
*Praise Him, Praise Him*
*Praise Him when the sun goes down*

We come from a long history of praying and praising people. As Catholic Christians, we have a rich prayer tradition. As people of African descent, it was the experience of our God as expressed in our prayer that allowed us to make a way out of no way. It was our belief that God truly hears our prayer that gave us hope in times of hopelessness, that guided us in times of darkness and that strengthened us in times of weakness. We believe that Jesus hears our prayers, and we believe that Mary and all the saints intercede on our behalf. We believe that prayer is the rising of one's mind and heart to God or the requesting of good things from God.[1] Because we believe in a good God, we praise and thank our God in the morning, in the noontime and when the sun goes down!

As African American people, our prayer has been a source of hope, guidance and strength. We have prayed on the mountaintop—as the Rev. Dr. Martin Luther King, Jr., expressed. We have prayed down low as our enslaved ancestors in the hush harbors prayed for their freedom from slavery. We have prayed in periods of isolation and desolation, as well as during periods of immense joy. Even during times of trouble, we have prayed and believed in the goodness of our God. Our prayer has been a source of deep spiritual release as well as a source of strength and power.

As Christians we state that we are followers and disciples of Jesus Christ. Jesus has been our model for prayer. He prayed in public and in private. He prayed as the trusting Son of the Father. He prayed in times of distress as well as in times of great joy. Examples of his prayer can be found in his baptism (Mark 1:9-11), at the Transfiguration (Mark 9:2-8), as well as in the Lord's Prayer (Matthew 6:9-13, Luke 11:2-4). The early church prayed daily, constantly, in community as well as individually, at home, in the synagogue and the temple, and even along the road. In the Acts of the Apostles, the apostle Philip was led by the Spirit to encounter the Ethiopian Eunuch, who after being baptized, rejoiced in prayer. Christian people come from a tradition of prayer, which has taken many forms over the ages. We review here the various forms of Christian prayer and reflect on the uses of these prayers in the formation and shaping of the spiritual life of African American Catholics.

### Forms of Christian Prayer

The *Catechism of the Catholic Church* states that God tirelessly calls each person to this mysterious encounter with Himself [Godself].[2] As Christians we believe that the heart is the place of encounter with God, the place of our covenant with God. Christian prayer, as the

*Catechism* explains, is our covenant relationship between God and man [woman] in Christ. It is the action of God and of humans, springing forth from the Holy Spirit and ourselves, wholly directed to the creator God in union with the human will of the Son of God made man. This action takes various forms: blessing and adoration, petition, intercession, thanksgiving and praise.

### PRAYER OF BLESSING AND ADORATION

The prayer of blessing is our response to God's gifts. Because God blesses us, we in turn can bless the One who is the source of every blessing.[3] One of our most common blessing prayers is the prayer we say before meals. We ask God to bless our food and the fellowship of our sharing. At the same time, through the prayer of adoration, we acknowledge, first, that we are created by God and also the greatness and the awesomeness of our God. You will note throughout *Songs of Our Hearts, Meditations of Our Souls* prayers of blessing and adoration.

### PRAYER OF PETITION

Prayers of petition are prayers in which we acknowledge our sinfulness, ask for God's forgiveness and express the need to turn back to our God. We are poor sinners who have turned away from God and now realize that we are in need of forgiveness. It is in fact the asking of forgiveness that shapes the first parts of this prayer and can be considered a prerequisite for all personal prayer in the Christian tradition. Christian prayers of petition also are prayers of trust, of a belief in a kingdom that will come and of a God who forgives, a God who will hear our prayer, if we pray in right mind and heart.

### PRAYER OF INTERCESSION

While prayers of petition are primarily focused on our own need for forgiveness and personal requests, prayers of intercession lead us to pray as Jesus did, on behalf of all others. Since the time of Abraham (when he interceded for the people of Sodom and Gomorrah), intercessory prayers have been characteristic of a heart attuned to God's mercy.[4] Since the church's beginnings, Christian intercession participates in Christ's intercession and reminds us of the communion of saints, who also intercede for us. As Christians we pray for all, even those who have done us harm.

### PRAYER OF THANKSGIVING

We thank God for everything. We thank God upon waking in the morning and before going to bed at night. God's goodness is cause enough for thanksgiving, but we remember that like the great Saint Paul, who also began and ended his prayers and letters with thanksgiving, we acknowledge that the Lord Jesus is always present to us. "In all circumstances give thanks, for this is the will of God for you in Christ Jesus."[5]

### PRAYER OF PRAISE

Praise is the form of prayer, which recognizes most immediately that God is God.[6] We praise God and give God glory because GOD IS. Praise in fact embraces all the other forms of prayer and carries them toward God who is the source and goal of our prayer.[7] An example of one of the earliest forms of this prayer is the doxology: Glory be to the Father, and to the Son, and to the Holy Spirit.

### PRAYER IN THE AFRICAN AMERICAN TRADITION

Prayer in the African American tradition has used all the beforementioned forms of prayer to express the relationship of Black people to their God. It is still common for African Americans to stop to invite God's blessing upon their food and fellowship before eating or celebrating. In prayer and in song, Black people have praised their God. Intercessory prayer can be seen when a person of African descent expresses the need of prayer: "Please pray for me." As well, it is not uncommon to hear someone from the African American community exclaim, "Thank you, Jesus!" We still get down on our knees to petition for forgiveness and pray for a change of heart.

Ultimately, prayer in the African American tradition has first and foremost been a conversation with God. The great religious leader, Sojourner Truth, is said to have claimed, "Children, I've talked with God. I've talked with Him in the woods and in the fields."[8] Without prayer, Black people would have perished in despair long ago, but the prayers of the people on the slave ships, in the fields, during the times of lynchings, gave them a common ground to continue to hope.[9] Prayers come from deep down in the soul and are the personal conversations that the individual and the community have with a loving God. This point is illustrated in a recent book about prayers in the African American community entitled *Conversations with God.*[10] James Melvin Washington states:

> African American prayers as a literary genre, and a religious social practice, assume that God is just and loving, and that the human dilemma is that we cannot always experience and see God's justice and love. We pray for faith to trust God's ultimate disclosure.[11]

Because these prayers are conversations, this means that for many African Americans, prayers do not have to be written down on paper in order to be invoked. A spontaneous approach to prayer is not uncommon in the community and can be evidenced when one enters into many Black Catholic churches during the prayers of the faithful, where prayers are elicited from the assembly. The challenge even with this collection of prayers was that while our community has a rich history of prayer, these prayers have primarily been invoked in a spontaneous manner and until recently, have not been written or collected.

Black prayer has been a vital force of liberation for African Americans because it invites free expression of the mind, soul and heart and historically has been a part of the spiritual empowerment of African Americans.[12] Through prayer, the individual and community gain a power that propels them to go forth and believe that "they can do all things through Christ." The prayer tradition furthermore expresses the ultimate faith the praying person and community had with God's action. The community participates in the prayers vocally but also by the swaying of their bodies, the raising of their hands and the nodding of their heads. Prayer in the Black community connects the individual and the community with the Divine.

### HOW TO USE THIS PRAYER BOOK

While there have been several books written on the prayer tradition of African Americans, this is the first book to address the prayer tradition of African American Catholics. As was stated earlier, prayer has been an important aspect of the spirituality of African American peoples. As Catholics of African descent, our prayer is also shaped by our Roman Catholic tradition. Note that the prayers within the book not only contain many traditional Catholic prayers but also prayers that address the unique experience of being an African American—racism, the importance of family, the challenge of HIV/AIDS.

In today's busy society it is a challenge just to find the time to pray. We may have the urge to pray and articulate the importance of prayer, but as the *Catechism of the Catholic Church* states, prayer cannot be reduced to just the spontaneous outpouring of an interior impulse, one also must have the will to pray and knowledge about how to pray. While the Holy Spirit teaches the children of God how to pray, our church has always offered models and help to those who are willing to become seekers.

The challenge for those of us in the African American Catholic community is that most prayer books do not address the unique needs of our community. This book has many traditional Catholic prayers such as the rosary, Hail Mary and Peace Prayer of Saint Francis, as well as original prayers by members of the African American Catholic community.

We have divided prayers into five sections. There are prayers of celebration and thanksgiving, prayers for children, prayers to the ancestors, prayers for facing problems and prayers for healing which all originate from the deep spiritual wells of African American Catholics and the rich prayer tradition of the Catholic church.

It is important to remember that we come from a scriptural tradition, and therefore the reading of sacred Scripture should accompany our prayer so that a dialogue takes place between God and man [all].[13] Several years ago, at a Catholic conference the workshop facilitator asked attendees to "take out our Bibles." She wished for us to look up a passage that she was describing. Unfortunately, most participants did not have their Bibles with them. The presenter admonished us and told us that we should have the Holy Scriptures with us at all times because we should always be ready to access the Word in our daily lives and encounters. If we do not know the Word of God, she asked, how can we preach, teach and model that Word in our daily lives?

Therefore, *Songs of Our Hearts, Meditations of Our Souls* should best be used as a companion to daily prayer with Scripture and participation in the Eucharist. You will note in the section on traditional prayers that we have included scriptural passages with the rosary prayers.

The section of the book entitled "This Little Light of Mine" is specifically appropriate for use with children and youth. These prayers may be helpful in teaching children about prayer and how to pray.

The editors of *Songs of Our Hearts, Meditations of Our Souls* composed the book in such a way that you will find not only prayers for private reflection and meditation, but also prayers that can be used in a communal setting. As you review the prayers in the book, you might find a prayer that speaks specifically to your current spiritual experience. You also might find a prayer that will encourage you in your ongoing relationship with God. There is no particular format except for you to find the time daily for ongoing prayer. Keep the prayer book by your bedside or take it with you on the bus or train while going to work. Some of our best prayer experiences may occur while traveling to and from work. You might also find the book helpful for planning and preparing prayer for communal settings. Many prayers are highly suitable to open and close such gatherings as meetings, days of reflection, prayer breakfasts and retreats.

The prayers in *Songs of Our Hearts, Meditations of Our Souls* not only reflect the beauty and richness of the prayer tradition in the African American Catholic community, but they also will help facilitate your own conversation with God.

C. Vanessa White, D. MIN.

## NOTES

[1] St. John Damascene, *De fide orth.* 3,24:PG 94, 1089C, as quoted in the *Catechism of the Catholic Church,* article 2559, p. 613.

[2] *Catechism of the Catholic Church,* 2591, p. 623.

[3] *Catechism of the Catholic Church,* 2626, p. 632.

[4] *Catechism of the Catholic Church,* 2635, p. 634.

[5] 1 Thessalonians 5:18.

[6] *Catechism of the Catholic Church,* 2639, p. 635.

[7] *Catechism of the Catholic Church,* 2639, p. 635.

[8] O. Richard Bowyer, Betty L. Hart, and Charlotte A. Meade, *Prayer in the Black Tradition* (Nashville, Tenn.: The Upper Room, 1986), p. 17.

[9] Carlyle Fielding Stewart, *Soul Survivors* (Louisville, Ky.: Westminster John Knox Press, 1997), p. 116.

[10] James Melvin Washington, PH.D., ed., *Conversations with God: Two Centuries of Prayers by African Americans* (New York: Harper Collins Publishers, 1994), p. xlvi.

[11] Ibid.

[12] Stewart, p. 116.

[13] *Catechism of the Catholic Church*, 2653, p. 637.

# PART ONE

**GYE NYAME**

# "I Know There's a God Somewhere"

## Prayers of Praise; Petitions and Meditations on the Goodness of God

> *Up over my head, I hear music in the air*
> *Up over my head, I hear music in the air*
> *Up over my heard, I hear music in the air.*
> *I know there's a God somewhere.*[1]

This is a lilting and meditative spiritual. Whoever sings it expresses his or her faith in a good, loving, gracious and ubiquitous God who cares for all and watches over all people and over all creation. Full of praise for such a glorious God, the singer responds to God in the way that God makes himself known to the singer through song and music. In *The Confessions*, Saint Augustine said restlessness was the lot of all people until they found their rest in God. When generations of enslaved African Americans sang "I Know There's a God Somewhere," they declared that despite their condition they were confident that God was a constant presence of goodness and mercy in their lives—for this God required their praise and thanksgiving which they offered unstintingly.

Passed down with care through the years, we still sing our praises to God, for it is right and fitting that we do so. When we raise our voices in praise with songs such as "I Know There's a God Somewhere," we give God the only gift we truly can give—our oblations of love and awe.

This section of *Songs of Our Hearts, Meditations of Our Souls* presents many different kinds of prayers, poems and meditations of praise as well as petitions for God's grace in our lives. We have chosen the much-beloved and probably the most commonly used and most readily recognized Adinkra symbol, *Gye Nyame,* to represent these prayers. It is used in vestments, in stained-glass windows, on pews and on altar linens in many African American Catholic parishes throughout the United States and also widely in its native land, Ghana. *Gye Nyame* means "except for God." Except for God we would be lost, we would be impoverished, we would be lonely, we would be restless. Except for God none merits praise and thanksgiving. Except for God we would not know goodness and grace. God created us, God is always with us, and God's love for us is without end. That is what the *Gye Nyame* reminds us of and that is what these prayers affirm.

Cecilia A. Moore, PH.D.

**NOTE**

[1] Traditional Spiritual.

## Sweet Holy Spirit

Sweet, sweet Holy Spirit—
Our Sanctifier and Giver of wonderful gifts.
Please bathe, saturate, imbue us
With Your graces, Your gifts and fruits
With Your blessings, Your love and forgiveness.
That we may give Praise, Honor and Glory to You,
Now and forever. Amen.

## Morning Prayer

My Jesus, thank you
For another day.
Lead me, guide me
Keep me in your way.

If I should stray
Show not your wrath,
But place me firmly
Back on the Path.

If I should fall
Show not your heel,
But show me your cross.
Make me feel what you feel.

And as I go
Through this gift filled day.
May it all be for you,
The Truth, the Life and the Way.

## No Certain Time, No Certain Place
### to Praise the Lord and See His Face

Some say they need to pray,
At a certain time or place
I say to praise the Lord always,
To see him face to face

When I wake up in the morning,
Blessed to see another day
I say to myself,
My Lord is here,
And he is having me, his way

As I carry on my business,
Confronting what the day may bring,
I silently shout "Hallelujah,"
And in my heart I sing

I tackle life's daily problems,
Without any feelings of unease,
For I know my Lord is with me,
Even if I don't fall upon my knees

Some say they need to pray,
At a certain time or place
I say to praise the Lord always,
To see him face to face

He should be praised, morn, noon, and night
Because he's real, though out of sight
This is that thing we call faith,
You only need it the size of a seed,
For his love to be omnipresent, for his love to be guaranteed

I praised him when I buried,
My father and my mother
I see him now as always, in the eyes
Of my sisters and my brothers

I see him in the face of a stranger
His love comforts me,
In the grasp of mortal danger

I praise him when I see the smile
of the one that I love
I praise him because she's a gift to me,
A special blessing from above

Some say they need to pray,
At a certain time or place
I say to praise the Lord always,
And you'll see him face to face

I know he'll never leave my side
So my love for him
Won't wait, it won't hide

If need be,
I'll shout it from a mountain
For my praise for him is continuous,
Like an ever-flowing fountain

I praise him when,
I retire for the evening, realizing all that he has done

I thank and praise
The Lord again
For Jesus, his only begotten son

As I close my eyes at night
Reliving all God's love for me
I dream and reflect on God's promise,
His promise of eternity

My Lord, My God
My Savior, My Jesus
You saved me with,
Your loving grace

I commit myself to you,
Right now,
No certain time,
No certain place

So praise him while you're in the car
And praise him while you play at the lake
Don't wait for an invitation
The enemy's bait, don't take
There is no need to set aside
A certain time for prayer
I praise him in the morning, noon, and night
I praise him everywhere

Some say they need to pray,
At a certain time or place
I say to praise the Lord always,
And you'll see him face to face

## Evening Prayer

Thank you, Jesus for another day
I hope I've pretty much kept on your way.
But if somehow I've caused you sorrow,
I'll try to do much better tomorrow.

Guard me as I sleep through the night,
And bring me through to morning light.
Bless my family and bless my friends,
And help us all work towards your ends.

And when our days are done
May we rise with you, his risen Son.


## Self-Sacrifice

All I want, all I feel, all I experience…
Comes from you.
Only you.
You give me Life, Hope, Faith, Inspiration, Love…
Life to live to its fullest, in order to more fully serve you.
Hope for the future, for the present, for the past, what is and
    what isn't.
Faith in you, in myself, in others, in what is to come.
Inspiration to do and say and write what comes from my heart,
    my soul.
Love for others, love for myself, love for you.
God, you give me everything, and in return…
I give myself to you.

## Prayer for Black Catholic Men

Let us pray!

"…the men should pray, lifting up holy hands…."
(1 Timothy 2:8)

Heavenly Father, Wonderful and Glorious God, your wonders work miracles. Your miracles work wonders in every moment of our lives. You are the Father of all compassion and the Mother of all creation. We bless you, we love you, we praise you for your glory. Enable us, dear Lord, to worship you in spirit and in truth.

We thank you for the great things that you've done, those wonderful things that you are doing even as we speak and for the glorious things that you will do in us, for us, and most significantly through us in the future.

Thank you Lord, for the Power of the Holy Spirit, which has protected, directed, provided and kept the Black Catholic man from the beginning of time to now. Endow us with the spirit of Augustine, the father of our theology, Popes Victor, Gelasius and Miltiades, the steadfastness and immovable resolve of the faith of the African Martyrs in Europe and in Africa. Teach us, Lord, about all the Black Catholic men in this country, lay and priest, whose fortitude, perseverance and unshakable love for you produces in us today, men who can finally worship you in our own tradition.

Lord, we thank you for dispelling all fear from our lives and replacing it with a God kind of faith, not just faith in God but the faith of God.

For no eye has seen, no ear has heard, no heart or mind can
conceive of the things that you have prepared for those
of us who love you. Amen.

## Words and Wisdom

I look for eloquence in words, to express my praise
And polysyllable words to express my joy.
But though I search for weeks and days,
I cannot find them, and I buoy
My soul with wonders words can't trace.
Because so wondrous are you, Lord,
That all the words of men
can never comprehend
The majesty of your love, the power of your grace.

So then, I look for knowledge—
The who, the where, the why,
The reason Someone great as you,
For me would suffer and die.

But I know that knowledge sought by men like me
Of why your love and mercy is so great
And spent so freely doesn't even hold the key
To why for us you bore Calvary's weight.

The answer is quite simple.
Only you can know
The depths of our ingratitude
And still help us to grow
To love you even in our ignorance.
For your love is so vast
It has no bounds, thus always flows.
And we are blessed to be in its path.

## Alphabet Prayer

A—Alpha, Almighty

B—Burden Bearer

C—Calm in a storm

D—Deliverer from oppression

E—Eternal, Everlasting God

F—Father, Faithful and merciful

G—God and lover of my soul

H—Holy, Heart fixer, and mind regulator

I—I, a sinner, need your

J—Justice, your Joy unspeakable

K—King of Kings

L—Lord of Lords

M—Merciful, Mighty God and Father

N—Nobody knows the troubles I've seen

O—Omega, Our Father always first and last

P—Prayers of the righteous and Purpose, we lift them up

Q—Quality and Quiet time is yours

R—Righteousness of Royal estate

S—Savior, bring Salvation from on high

T—Trusting in your Word alone

U—Use me to do your will

V—Victory can be mine through you

W—World Without end

X—X-out all that is not of God

Y—You, oh Lord, oh God of my salvation

Z—Zion, our home on high. Amen, Amen, Amen.

## Footprints

One night a man had a dream. He dreamed he was walking along the beach with the LORD. Across the sky flashed scenes from his life. For each scene, he noticed two sets of footprints in the sand; one belonged to him, and the other to the LORD.

When the last scene of his life flashed before him, he looked back at the footprints in the sand. He noticed that many times along the path of his life there was only one set of footprints. He also noticed that it happened at the very lowest and saddest times in his life.

This really bothered him and he questioned the LORD about it. "LORD, you said that once I decided to follow you, you'd walk with me all the way. But I have noticed that during the most troublesome times in my life, there is only one set of footprints. I don't understand why when I needed you most you would leave me."

The LORD replied, "My precious, precious child, I love you and I would never leave you. During your times of trial and suffering, when you see only one set of footprints, it was then that I carried you."

## Butterfly

The caterpillar slows down, stops
moving about, knowing it must make a
change: Metamorphoses.
Out of the cocoon comes the
butterfly: God's liberation of beauty.
Sit still so that God can make the
change in you, then fly and share
God's beauty.

## Paradise

Twenty-four years
And several kingdoms ago
I was a psalm

Undaunted men sang their praises
The words of hymn carried off by the wind
Then rapt in my arms and stood still

My empire was built with a grain of sand
A pebble from the road where Jesus' cross fell
The point where the Earth split and Man divided

Tears of a nation poured into the ridges
Waters that flooded the earthen cracks
Then brought Man back together once again

Paradise was not so unknown then
For it could be seen through the eyes of a child
Never mind that cross or His mother's tear-streaked face

The Father watched as His Son walked that road then
     was reconciled
Because His unworthy nation cursed at first
But then followed

## He IS

If my love for Him
Could be measured
It would reach as high
As that tower in Babel
And deep as the river's bend

I'd call out to Him even
When my voice remains
But a whisper
My prayers, sweet vibrations
That begin as thoughts
And smash into one another
To form words on my tongue

I'd close my eyes at night
And see Him still
Even when I think
He might not want
To be there

But I will know He IS
Because the simple fact
That I wake in the morning
Would remind me
That no one could ever
Love me the way that He does
No one ever will

## The Path

I make my way down a crooked path. It is dark and perilous,
the only path I have ever known…. The words of my mother
stay with me in needful times, moments, especially like these. I
close my eyes tightly then hear them: muffled at first and then
clearly. I allow them to resound over and over, again and
again…until nothing can be heard but these professions in the
still of night. Twenty-four years later, I remember the prayer
exactly the way she taught it to me. And I imagine my peace. I
begin "The Lord's Prayer." And I am moved.

The words to that prayer stay with me, and I remember where I
came from. My ancestors have trod this path many times before;
they have seen this same darkness. The spirit of the ancestors
rise within me, calming my fears and appeasing my soul. Their
words coerce me into doing the unthinkable. They have crossed
rivers and fed multitudes with nothing, so I can find my way. If
the removal of God's curse was the sacrifice of His only son
nailed to a cross, then what good does my sacrifice do? I turn to
face Him then, not because I am ready, but because it is time.

The Lord hisses softly into my ears and tells me not to be afraid.
His hands gently push me farther down that path until I see a
light. I have gone so long in the darkness that at first, I do not
recognize this light. When it seems that I have gone too far,
everything stops. The Lord smiles down upon me, and I can feel
that light tingling in my bones. There are so many things I want
to say to Him then but not enough words to express them.
Slowly, I piece myself back together like a puzzle, and I find,
among the remains, pieces of Him. I will take the Lord with me
wherever I may go. I hope that He will take me as well.

# PART TWO

**AKOMA**

# "This Little Light of Mine"
## Prayers for Children and Families

While almost anyone can easily join in a rollicking rendition of "This Little Light of Mine," only a few will readily recognize it as an African American spiritual. Most of us learn the song early in life in preschool, kindergarten, or in Sunday school. Its simple lyrics and singsong tune make it easy to learn and fun to sing. "This Little Light of Mine" is also a favorite song to teach children because it affirms the goodness that God has planted in the soul of each person. This is the goodness that shines so naturally in children. This goodness is the Light of God.

*This little light of mine, I'm gonna let it shine. This little light of mine, I'm gonna let it shine. Let it shine, let it shine, let it shine.*

*My Lord gave it to me, I'm gonna let it shine. My Lord, gave it to me, I'm gonna let it shine. Let it shine, let it shine, let it shine.*

*Hide it under a barrel, no, I'm gonna let it shine. Hide it under a barrel, no, I'm gonna let it shine. Let it shine, let it shine, let it shine.*[1]

When children sing this spiritual, they boldly proclaim their knowledge that God made them, that they are valuable, and that they have a responsibility to show their goodness and share their gifts with the world.

We have chosen this spiritual as the meditation song for these prayers for children and families because in traditional African societies and in African American culture, children are regarded as the most important gifts of God and as the wealth of a family. They are the light of the family and bring goodness to all in the family. In this section of the prayer book, you will find prayers for children and parents, a Franciscan meal blessing, a baptismal prayer and a First Communion prayer, a family reunion prayer, a prayer for students, and prayers for those who work with youth and that attend to concerns of families.

The Adinkra symbol we have chosen for this section is the *Akoma*. The *Akoma* looks like a heart and is often translated as "the heart." In Western culture the heart symbolizes love. The *Akoma* symbolizes patience and tolerance. If we blend the meaning of the heart symbol with the meanings of the *Akoma*, we have the principal ingredients necessary for happy and blessed children and families: love, patience and tolerance.

Cecilia A. Moore, PH.D.

**NOTE**

[1] Traditional Spiritual.

## Prayer for African American Families

Lord, here we are—sons and daughters of Africa who yearn to walk in the ways of Jesus. Bless our families in which you have placed us. Bless our ancestral and extended families all over Africa. Help us to recognize that we are indeed strength for each other. Keep us ever close to you, O Lord, and if we lose our way, bring us back, O Lord. Keep us ever mindful of the Scriptures remembering that "when two or three of us are gathered—you shall stand with us." Help us to pass on to the next generations the gifts you have given us and the generations before us—the gift of Jesus, the gift of faith, the gift of genius, the gift of strength and the gifts of pride and courage. Help us to continue to stretch out our hearts and hands to each other— remembering the old African proverb that says, "One single bracelet does not jingle alone." Help us, Lord, for all things are possible through you. This we ask in Jesus' name. Amen.

## Prayer for African American Families

GOD OF MERCY AND GOD
OF LOVE we place our African
American families before you
today. May we be proud of our
history and never forget those
who paid a great price for our
liberation. Bless us one by one
and keep our hearts and minds
fixed on higher ground. Help us to
live for you and not for ourselves,
and may we cherish and proclaim
the gift of life. Bless our parents,
guardians, grandparents,
relatives and friends. Give us the
amazing grace to be the salt of the
earth and the light of the world.
Help us, as your children, to live
in such a way that the beauty and
the greatness of authentic love is
reflected in all that we say and
do. Give a healing anointing to
those who are less fortunate,
especially the motherless, the
fatherless, the broken, the sick
and the lonely. Bless our departed
family members and friends. May
they be led into the light of your
dwelling place where we will
never grow old, where we will
share the fullness of redemption

and shout the victory for all
eternity. This we ask in the
precious name of Jesus, our
Savior and Blessed Assurance.
Amen.

Holy Mother of God, pray for us.

## Prayer for African American Families...in the Times of Trouble

O Lord our God, our family stands in the need of prayer for
there is trouble brewing in our midst.
    We've been tossed and driven.
    We've been bound in misery.
We've been in dark halls and slippery places.
We've been wounded and our pain is deep.
So, we've sought shelter under that which is greater than
    ourselves
For you alone are willing and able.

Help us, Lord, to look up to thee, so that we can get up out of
    this misery.
Help us, Lord, to hear your call in our night of despair,
    "Lo, I am with you."

Help us, Lord, for all things are possible through you who
    strengthen
both the weak and the brave alike.
Help us, Lord, for in the time of trouble our only victory is
    the victory
won by your mercy and your grace. This we ask in the
precious name of Jesus. Amen.

## Family Reunion Prayer

We thank you, Father
for your love and grace.

We thank you, Father
for the family members
gathered for this family reunion.

We thank you, Father
for the healing of hearts
as we remember
family shepherded into your
kingdom.

We thank you, Father
for our family that could not come,
for our church families near and far,
for our many friends,
for everyone who gave so
unselfishly of time and talent
in celebration of family.

We humbly thank you, Father
for this day
renew our spiritual lights
lead us in your way
order our steps
according to your will.

We thank you, Father
as we travel to our homes
guide us safely
throughout each day.

We give you glory and praise, Father
We ask these prayers
In the name of your son, Jesus,
We thank you, Father.

## A Father's Prayer

Dear Lord,

I love you Lord. I give you thanks and praise. I come before you today to pray for my children.

I ask you to give them the strength they may need to overcome hardships. I pray that they will be able to recognize what is good and appreciate the good that happens to them in life.

I pray that they will understand that all that they have comes from you. I pray that they will recognize the gifts you have given them and be willing to share their gifts with others in return.

Lord, let me be attentive to what they are telling me. Guide me so that I may seek the best ways to help and advise them.

I ask these things in the name of your Son, Jesus Christ. Amen.

## Prayer of a Mother

Good and gracious God,

You are the source of all love. You are the source of all grace. I humbly come before you to thank you for choosing to make me a mother. Help me to be worthy of that choice. Help me to appreciate each child as your precious gift to our family.

Give me your guidance so that I may be an example of a faith-filled woman and mother. Help me to teach my children about you and your love for them. Help me to teach them that they are precious in your sight and that you are always with them. Guide me in teaching them the Catholic faith. Help me to make our home sacred space.

Give me patience so that I may discipline them appropriately. Give me wisdom to answer their questions. Help me to continue to trust that you will provide for us.

When my strength and energy are low, let me be mindful that you are a source of refreshment. When I am troubled, let me not forget the comfort to be found in you. When there is illness in the family, help me maintain my trust in you and accept your will.

When all is well, I thank you. When things are not going well, I thank you. I thank you for what you have shown and taught me thus far.

I ask you to watch over my family and to keep them from all hurt, harm and danger.
Lord, help me to be the mother you wish me to be.

I ask this in the name of Jesus, your Son. Amen.

## A Scripture to Inspire You as You Teach

On Saturday evening we gathered together for the fellowship meal. Paul spoke to the people and kept on speaking until midnight, since he was going to leave the next day. Many lamps were burning in the upstairs room where we were meeting. A young man named Eutychus was sitting in the window, and as Paul kept on talking, Eutychus got sleepier and sleepier, until he finally went sound asleep and fell from the third story to the ground. When they picked him up, he was dead. But Paul went down and threw himself on him and hugged him. "Don't worry," he said, "he is still alive!" Then Paul went back upstairs, broke bread and ate. After talking with them for a long time, even until sunrise, Paul left. They took the young man home and were greatly comforted. (Acts 20:7-12)

## Prayer to Guardian Angel

Angel of God, my Guardian dear,
To whom God's love commits me here;
Ever this day be at my side,
To light and guard, to rule and guide.
Amen.

## Angel Prayer

Angels—Spiritual beings
   Sent by God.
Please guard, guide and
   Protect *(name)*.
And those who come
   Across our paths
In thought, in spirit
   And
In physical presence.
   Amen.

## A Prayer for Catechists and Youth Ministers as You Teach

Lord God, we hear you saying to *keep on teaching until the dead come back to life again*. We thank you for calling us into this mighty ministry.

Walk with us, Lord, so that we may know the path that you want us to take.
Keep watch over our hearts so that we may share your word in spirit and in truth. Give us a well-trained tongue so that we may proclaim the whole truth and
   nothing but the truth.

Stir our spirits and use us to lift up those who are trampled down upon. And finally, Lord, help us to remember that through Christ, you have given us what we want, given us what we need and have given us a new attitude to teach until the dead come back to life again. Amen.

## Prayer for Students

Dear Lord,
I call upon your precious name to give you the praise, the honor
and the glory.
Lord, I thank you
for my faith, family, finances, friends,
fitness and feelings. Lord, I
especially thank you for the gift of
life. Thank you for affording me the
opportunity to experience a gift that
my ancestors and forefathers dreamed of,
and prayed to you for. Lord, in those
tired moments, I ask that you give me
strength. In those moments of
confusion, I ask that you give me
clarity. In those moments of loneliness.
I ask that you give me comfort. And in
those stressful moments, I ask that you
give me peace. Lord, I thank you for
the gift of your Son, Jesus, without
whose sacrifices I would not be able to
enter into a peaceful everlasting life
with you. Help me, when times get
tough to focus on him, Lord. I ask all
of this in your precious, unmatchable,
holy name. Amen!

## Morning Prayer of Thanks

Good morning, Lord!
Thank you for the glory of the Sun.
Thank you for the health I have to get my duties done.
I shall devote the hours of this blessed day to you,
By honoring your holy name in everything I do.
I shall face my daily work without complaint or fear,
And make every effort to be friendly and sincere.
I know there have been many days I've wasted away;
But this one, I'll try to make your special day.
So once more, good morning, Lord, and please depend on me,
Because I want to honor you, through all eternity. Amen.

## Parents' Baptism Prayer

Lord Jesus, you have blessed us with our child, *Name*,
and brought us here to the waters of baptism.
Help *Name* to know you and bless you as Lord and savior.
Be our son's/daughter's light and help him/her to walk
    your Way.
Welcome *Name* to these waters of redemption, peace
    and freedom.
Wash him/her and welcome him/her as your own and
    make a place for him/her at the gracious banquet
    of your love. Amen.

## Prayer for the Blessing of Youth Councils

*(Ask congregation to extend their hands toward the young people)*

God of our ancestors, we call upon you right now. We ask that you extend a hand of blessing upon these young people who have assembled at the foot of the altar. Lord, we ask that you guide their programs and lives so that you may truly use them as instruments of your peace. Help their programs and ideas to come to fruition, and anything that the devil may try to raise up in their lives, we ask that you crush with your mighty hand. Lord, we also ask that you send a special blessing to all our young people and families here. May they get involved in the programs that we offer so that our church can benefit from the talents of all your children. We also ask that you bless the adults that work with our youth. We know that it is trying and taxing at times to deal with our youth, but Lord we ask that you give them strength and wisdom when they get weary and confused. Also, give them the foresight to know that you are in control when all seems lost. We ask this in your mighty name. And the church says Amen! Amen! Amen!

## Prayer for Those Who Work With Young People

Lord, let me do your will in whatever way you want to me do it.
As you know, I am the "Center of Alternative Programs."
I am surrounded by young people with many needs, collective
   and individual.
I ask you for your grace to answer this call in whatever way you
   want to respond.
Lord, guide me and direct me as I try to answer these young
   people in their call for help.
Lord, when I cannot impact these young people with words at
   least let me give them a good example.
I know that changes in behavior do not come overnight, but
   Lord, please let me see some changes that will allow me to
   continue to try to influence them with enthusiasm.
This special blessing I ask, Lord, in the name of your Son, Jesus.
Amen.

## First Communion Prayer

Here I am, Jesus!
I have waited for this day for such a long time.
Jesus, I believe in you and I love you.
I want to come to your table today
and enjoy the feast of your sacrament of love for us.
By receiving the gift of your body and blood,
Help me to know you better, to follow you more closely
and to love you more. Amen.

## Franciscan Mealtime Blessing

Praise the Lord,
The eyes of all look
To you Lord, and you give
Them their food in due season.
You open your hands and satisfy the desire of every
    living thing.

Let us pray...

+Bless us, O Lord,
and these, your gifts,
which we are about to receive,
through Jesus Christ, our Lord. Amen.

# PART THREE

AYA

# "Wade in the Water"

## Prayers for Life in the World

*Wade in the water*
*Wade in the water, children,*
*Wade in the water*
*God's a-going to trouble the water*[1]

Everywhere we look there is trouble. Hurricanes, fires, earth-quakes, tsunamis, droughts and floods cause untold suffering, displacement and pain throughout the world. Violence in our homes and neighborhoods destroys lives, families and communities.

Hypertension, diabetes, cancer and HIV/AIDS plague our people. Many suffer because their families are torn by divorce, dissention and poor communication. We often try to run away from our problems, to ignore them, or to simply pretend that we have no problems, not of our own making anyway. But running, ignoring and pretending change nothing.

The church teaches that we are never alone in facing our problems, and daily calls us to present our concerns and needs to God, to seek reconciliation with those who we have offended and with those who have offended us, and to trust that with God's help and grace and our determination to make things better and right, we will not fail.

Our enslaved ancestors knew this, trusted it and sang about it all of the time. Like all spirituals, "Wade in the Water" possesses layer upon layer of meaning and is derived from the experiences of the enslaved, their understanding of what it meant to be a child of God and their identification with God's people who throughout the ages trusted in God so much that they did not shrink from the trials and tribulations before them, but faced them confident that God would not let them fall.

"Wade in the Water" is the African American slaves' reflection on the saving action of God who delivered the Hebrews from bondage in Egypt. As God liberated the Hebrews from slavery and saw to their safe and miraculous passage through the Red Sea into freedom, these enslaved men and women believed without a doubt that God would do the same for them. Hence, the song beckons its hearer to trust in God, to get in the water that seems to teem with danger and to know that in troubling this water God will deliver his people.

This is a message that we all need today and that is why we have chosen this spiritual as the meditation for these prayers for life in the world. Here you will find prayers that address many of the troubles we face in the modern world, as well as prayers for people working to resolve problems and to serve those who are in need. We pray that like the beautiful spiritual, "Wade in the Water," those who pray these prayers will find the hope and confidence they need to ask for God's help and do what they can to make things better and right.

The *Aya* represents the fern plant and symbolizes endurance and resourcefulness. Ferns have the ability to grow and flourish in the most difficult of places. God's ability to see us through all the problems we face is like the fern. Though we do not see a way out, God does. Go ahead, wade in the water.

Cecilia A. Moore, PH.D.

## NOTE

[1] "God's A-Gwinter Trouble De Water" in *The Books of American Negro Spirituals: Including The Book of American Negro Spirituals and The Second Book of Negro Spirituals* by James Wheldon Johnson and J. Rosamond Johnson (New York: Viking Press, 1969) pp. 84-85.

## Call to Prayer

God of our ancestors,
You who are living and true,
hear our prayers as we come before you this day.
We come to give you thanks, O God,
for all that you are,
and for all that you do for us.
We praise you, we magnify you, we glorify you,
O Beauty ever-ancient, ever-new.
We come this day to also lift up those who suffer. . .
Be it spiritually, emotionally or physically.
We ask you, God ever-faithful,
to hear our prayers.
Restore your creation to its intended state.
Grant peace, harmony and health.
But not our will, O God, only yours be done.
For we make this prayer in faith
through Christ our Lord.
*All*: Amen.

## Hurricane Katrina Prayer of Consolation

O God our refuge and our strength, we come as humbly as we
know how, praying for our sisters and brothers affected and
effected by Hurricane Katrina.

**We need you right now, Lord of Life and Mercy.**

During these times be the God of our weary years and
silent tears.
Be our stronghold and deliverer.
In your great mercy, comfort those who suffer and grieve at
this very hour.

O Lord, grant life eternal to those who have fallen asleep
in death.
Wrap your mantle of grace and mercy around all of us.
Give us your divine staying power.
Lord God, infuse wisdom and understanding into the hearts,
minds and souls of those who seek to alleviate the pain and
anguish of the suffering.

**We need you right now, Lord of Life and Mercy.**

Holy Spirit, direct the paths of the future decisions to be made
for the Gulf Coast States and comfort those uprooted souls as
you plot a new course in their lives.
O Lord, hold our feeble hands and grant us protection from all
hurt, harm and danger.
Give us, Lord, what we need to lift up and build up one another
in faith, hope and love.
We ask all of these things in the precious name of your Son,
Jesus Christ, our Bread of Life.
Holy Mary, Mother of God,
Angels and Saints,
Be our intercessors.
Amen.

## Flood Waters

*In memory of those killed by Hurricane Katrina and those who survived*

Our lives are changed because of them;
There are so many floaters, so much saturation,
Yet we are not drenched out, if we have hope for one another.
These unwanted waters guide us.
They join the tributaries of the Mighty Mississippi
Who breathe aware of our loss and pain.
New Orleanians, we are from the living waters,
That others may sip from us (not knowing what they drink).
We quench their thirst so that
They may become fountains in which
Fresh water is contained.
We serve our loved ones
As sails serve the wind that propels the ship.
Our veins are our tributaries
The heart, our river.

## Prayer to the Gentle Healer

Gentle Healer, I have fallen on a shaky, rocky road and
momentarily lost my balance. The rocks in my way, please
let them be stepping stones; the worry lines in my brow, let
them be receptacles for your divine touch. My body is your
temple. Consecrate this temple and remove any uncleanness-
from it. Your Word never fails, cannot lie, will not go unheard.
Lift me with the strength to hold onto you and to trust, as I do,
that all is well. In your holy name, I pray. Amen!

## Prayer of Petition

O God, our help in ages past, our hope for years to come.

Father of all Creation, we humbly beseech you and ask mercy and forgiveness for all our sins and transgressions.

We haven't been all that we could be, but God we ask for strength in our weakness to break the grip that binds us to do what is not pleasing in thy sight.

Have mercy on us.

Bless us now, our country, our leaders, our families and all of our loved ones who serve our country abroad and at home.

Bless and keep their families and loved ones safe.

Lord, as we rise to face each new day, we're thankful for your new mercies.

Guide us, protect us and hold us in the hollow of your hands.

Until we meet again in Jesus' name, we pray in the name of the Father, Son and Holy Spirit. Amen, Amen, Amen.

## Prayer for Deliverance

Didn't you deliver Daniel, my Lord!
For ___, for each member of our family,
for every child we pray
for deliverance from the Lion's den
from addictions of every sort

We pray unceasingly and
take the authority that is ours as believers
to say NO
to every self-destructive evil
tendency or temptation
To say YES
to fullness of life

We have the courage
knowing ourselves
to love ourselves

We are vessels
seeking to be filled
with Your love
and mercy
and peace
acting to empty ourselves

We speak that love to the world
starting with those closest to us
in blood and in spirit. Amen.

## Prayer for Those Suffering From HIV/AIDS

God of our weary years,
God of our silent tears,
O Good and gracious God,
You are the God of health and wholeness.
In the plan of your creation,
You call us to struggle in our sickness
and to cling always to the cross of your Son.
Father, we are your servants.
Many of us are now suffering with HIV or AIDS.
We come before you, and ask you,
if it is your holy will,
to take away this suffering from us,
restore us to health and lead us to know you
and your powerful healing
love of body and spirit.
We ask you also,
to be with those of us who nurse your sick ones.
We are the mothers, fathers, sisters, brothers,
children and friends of your suffering people.
It is so hard for us to see those whom we love suffer.
You know what it is to suffer.
Help us to minister in loving care, support and
patience for your people who suffer with HIV and AIDS.
Lead us to do whatever it will take to
eradicate this illness from the lives of those
who are touched by it,
both directly and indirectly.
Trusting in you and the strength of your Spirit,
we pray these things in the name of Jesus. Amen.

## I'm Going Through

Difficult times and problems will not slay me—
   I'm going through.
Times may be rough and solutions not immediately at hand
   but I'm going through.
Times may be unsteady and answers only remotely discerned
   but I'm going through.

I have come too far to be turned around. I have
   prayed too long to be dismayed or turned around.
The bottom line states as strong as my heart's conviction
   can make it is—I'm going through.

My God who holds tomorrow in his hand and who will
   allow me to hold the edge of his garment,
My God will lead the way, and I can state with heart-
   felt conviction—no doubt of his love which is like
   pure gold—
My God and I are going through.

My faith may get a little tattered and ragged at the
   edges, but then he touches me ever so gently
   and with faith aglow and joy in my soul—
   gently I take up my cross and go through. Amen.

## Prayer for the National Gathering of Black Catholic Women

Wisdomwoman God,

As we gather by your power in the 21st century, we bring together our collective resonance of the beauty of life.

Because we are ceaselessly in touch with you and touched by you, our struggles against barriers which divide are transformed into intergenerational bondings which unite.

We have known joy and pain, and we are obliged to grace one another with the collective wisdom of journeys.

Permit us, Wisdomwoman God, to seize these days and nights and to be in sanctuary together where we tap into our untapped treasures which allow us to love you and to cause you to be loved.

We magnify you because, in times of strength our power is channeled; in times of weakness, your power is summoned.

Help us to continue to embrace our identity which we cannot escape and which cannot escape us: Intergenerational Black Catholic Women.

Give us the grace to pour out ourselves like good wine for the sake of your kingdom. Amen.

## Addict's Prayer

Heavenly Father, forgive me my past sins as a drug user; protect
my future; heal my sick body and mind.

Lord Jesus, hear my prayer for all drug users; heal us with your
love, give us the strength we need to reject the temptation
of drugs.

Loving Blessed Mother, pray for us and our mothers.

You know the heartache of watching a child suffer and you
know a mother's sorrow.

Dear Mother of our Lord Jesus, remember us, touch us with
your love and peace.

## A Prayer for Reconciliation

Hallowed be thy name
Whose tortured feet testify
To the power of the past.

Hallowed be thy breath
Whose cursed name bears
My silent reckonings.

Hallowed be thy love
Whose broken heart
Beats your lost child's secret:
her sacred name.

## Vocation Prayer

God our Liberator,
We thank you and praise you
For you are a God who walks with us,
Who knows our struggles,
And who gives us strength to answer your call.

You have created us in your likeness
…I hear you calling us
to greatness as servants of the Gospel.

You have brought us a mighty long way
…I hear you calling us to keep on keeping on.

You have anointed us to bring glad tidings to the poor
And to set captives free
…I hear you calling us to go
and tell the Good News about Jesus Christ.

You have blessed us with family and faith, spirit and soul
…I hear you calling us to live and leave a legacy of love.

"Oh my Lord, what shall I do?"

Free us, Faithful God, to hear your call.
Help us, Loving God, to hear your voice—
True, constant, full of hope, above so many others.
Empower us, Way-Maker God, to place our lives
In the service of our sisters and brothers.

With faith and unfailing confidence,
We ask this prayer through Jesus Christ your Son. Amen.

## Prayer for Vocations

Lord, you are a mighty good God!
I know I can count on you to never leave my side.
I've searched for your voice,
For your Blessed Assurance in my frenzied living,
But you were nowhere to be found.
So today I come to you in the quiet and the still
And ask you to speak to my heart
Help me hear your gentle whisper
So that I may know what you would have me to do.
Help me to trust your gentle whisper
That I may follow your will and not my own.
Sweet Jesus, you know I love you and I know that
You love me, too.
Show me now how you want me to serve
And I will be obedient.
I'm asking you as a brother, a friend,
As my Lord and Savior, Jesus Christ. Amen.

## Prayer for the Lost and Confused

Lost and confused. Find me, Lord. Make it clear.
Lost and confused. Hasten to me, Sweet Jesus.
Lost and confused. I cry out to God. Only He can save me from
the snare of despair and sorrow.
Lost and confused. God can!

## Prayer for Proper Use of Talents

Lord, let me use the talents you have given me for your honor and your glory.

Let me not get caught up in earthly travails.

Give me the wisdom to prioritize life as you, Lord, would have it to be.

Let me always be aware that people are more important than things, and we should never use people in a negative way in order to acquire things.

Lord, let me be supportive of people who want to make positive changes in their lives.

Lord, give me the grace to direct those entrusted to me or who ask my help as they seek you.

Let me be your instrument, Lord.

Let me always use the proper words, take the proper actions and always give the proper example.

For these blessings, I pray. Amen.

## Prayer for Those Seeking God

Lord, here I am, trying to make my way to you.

I pray that I follow your lead.

I pray that I move past all those things that keep me from you.

I do realize that I cannot do that without you.

God, my center, here I am, trying to make my way to you.

## A Prayer for Social Justice

Let us pray!

Gracious Father, you are a Mighty and Good God who showers us with your blessings. You not only fill our cup, but make it overflow! Yet we live in a world so much less generous than you. We live in a world that hoards the goods of the earth; a world of first worlds and third worlds; a world of haves and have-nots; of prosperity and poverty. We live in a world where it can be a crime to "drive while black" and a misdemeanor to defraud while white; where drug use is a criminal offense if black and only a sickness if white; a jail sentence for one and six months of rehab for the other. Lord, you said that if we hunger and thirst for justice, we will be satisfied! Hear our prayer, oh God, your people are hungry for justice to roll down like waters and righteousness like a mighty stream, as Isaiah and Martin prayed. But God remind us that all justice begins with our relationship with you. If justice is to give what is one's due, then show us where we fail to give you your due. For the times you called us to stand up and lead our families and we didn't; for the times you asked us to be there for our children and we weren't; for the times you asked us to be a source of encouragement for our wives and we broke their spirit and demeaned their worth; for the times you asked us to practice what we preached in our pulpits and we refused. Oh Lord, today we ask not only for justice, but for mercy; mercy for our failure to do justice, and mercy for those who fail to extend justice to us. Oh Just Father, have mercy! Amen!

## Prayer for Guidance

Lead me. Guide me.
Your will not mine, Lord.
Lead me. Guide me.
I don't know the way.
I've tried stepping out on my own and I just mess things up.
Lead me. Guide me.
Your will, Lord, not mine.

## Prayer for Those Who Are Suffering

When we are suffering, we forget that someone else is also
   suffering.
Our sorrow looms so large that it often blinds us to another.
Lord God, help me to focus on your love and kindness,
   so that I can joyfully do what you ask.

## Prayer Haiku

Listening to my Lord
Turning over all worries
Enjoying the peace

## An African Prayer

O God, you gave us life and we are here.

> We are here!

The cows and the land are here.

> They are here!

Milk and sorghum are here.

> They are here!

The sun rises over the mountain each morning.

> It rises. It is here!

We thank you for all your gifts, O loving God.

> We thank you!

Send us rain so that our crops will grow
and we and our cows can drink.

> Send us rain!

Give us laughing children to care for and to
train in the ways of our people.

> Give us children!

Put respect in the hearts of our boys and girls
for all human life and for the earth.

> Give them respect!

Let our old men and women be wise and
  make us open to their wisdom.

                                    Give us wisdom!

Let us hold on to the ways you taught us
  through our Brother, Jesus.

                                    May we keep them!

Let us care for our brothers and sisters with
  love as Jesus loves us.

                                    May we love them!


Take away the guns that kill our children.

                                    Take them away!

Take away the violence that disrupts our cities.

                                    Take it away!

Take away the fear that leads our people to violence.

                                    Take it away!

Take away the poverty and homelessness that lead
  to disease and despair.

                                    Take them away!


Give us hope, that we may believe in the possibility
  of peace when surrounded by cynicism.

                                    Give us hope!

Give us courage, that we may live what we believe
    when surrounded by ridicule.

                                                    Give us courage!

Give us selflessness, that we may care about
    others even when the costs are great.

                                                    Give us selflessness!


You taught us through your life and through
    your death.

                                                    You taught us!

You call us each day to enter into your life and to
    share your death.

                                                    You call us!

You call us each day to learn from others by
    sharing their lives and their deaths.

                                                    You call us!

May we teach others about you through our
    lives and our deaths.

                                                    May we teach!

*All:* Listen to us, aged God,
Listen to us, ancient God,
Who has ears.

Look at us, aged God,
Look at us, ancient God,
Who has eyes.

Receive us, aged God,
Receive us, ancient God,
Who has hands.

We praise you!
We thank you!
We glorify you!
Amen! Amen! Amen!

## Prayer for Choirs, Choir Directors, Ministers of Music and Musicians

Heavenly Father,

You have gifted your people, who have sprung from the continent of Africa, with a Gift of Music that has been used to give you praise.

We thank you, Lord, for the ability to use our gifts to communicate Black Sacred Song so that it evangelizes all who hear the Good News that you are our God and you love us ALL unconditionally.

May the spirits of our ancestors, including Fr. Clarence Joseph Rivers, Leon Roberts, James Weldon Johnson, Thomas Dorsey, Harry Burleigh, Mahalia Jackson, Mary Lou Williams and the patron saint of music, Saint Cecilia, be with us as we minister to your people here on earth.

We ask this through our Lord Jesus Christ, your Son, who lives and reigns with you and the Holy Spirit, one God, for ever and ever. Amen.

## Prayer for Solidarity and Steadfastness in Ministry

Here we are, Lord, gathered together around your holy throne, united in prayer and standing in one accord. We know that you have called us—and we know "how beautiful are the feet of those who announce good news." We thank you, Lord. We praise you, Lord, for you continue to give us gifts which we cannot give to ourselves. We call upon you this day, for we remember, "if God is for us who can be against us." We come before you this day, remembering our ancestors' work of unity and steadfastness because "it takes many hands to put a roof onto a hut." With you, O Lord—ain't no stopping us now. We know Lord, that you have already done great things for us and holy is your name. Ain't no stopping you, O Lord, for you provided us rest during the night and you gave us Jesus to bring rest to us during the day. Ain't no stopping you, Lord, for you hold the present and the future in the palm of your hand. East or west, north or south cannot contain what you can do and what you will do. You have redeemed us and called us by name to be yours. You, O God, are everything we want, everything we need and everything that is good. We praise you for bringing us here right now to do your will, to do your work. And know this day, O Lord, that we recognize that you want us to "keep on, keeping on" and we done made our vow, Lord, and bless us as we step up and step forward with you. This we ask in Jesus' name. Amen.

## Prayer for Discernment for Black Catholic Leaders

Good and Gracious God,
As a people on a journey
Help us to be open to your Spirit,
That Spirit, which moved our ancestors to be persons
Of deep faith and action.
Give us a discerning spirit
To help us to be attentive to
Your presence and to make that
Presence known and real in our communities.
We pray in the name of Jesus, and through the power
of the Holy Spirit.
Amen.

## Fear Not

Be not afraid
He is at your side

Be not afraid
He is with you

Be not afraid
He will assist you

Believe in Him
Christ the Lord

And

You will have nothing to fear

Fear Not

## Prayer for Unity in Evangelization Ministry

Most Holy God, through your abundant grace and mercy, you have fashioned a way for us to gather together united with you in spirit and in heart. We praise you Father, Son and Holy Spirit for you are an awesome God who can make the crooked places straight, and you continue to bring salvation and victory to your people. United in mind and in heart, we seek a new day of blessings from you, O Lord, as we journey as church into the future. United in mind and in heart we seek your blessing to strengthen our hands so that we may build where you want us to build. United in mind and in heart we seek your blessing to give us well-trained tongues so that we may teach and preach the good news of Jesus Christ. United in mind and in heart we seek your blessing to move our feet to the place where you want us to be. United in mind fill our hearts with compassion so that our love for you will govern what we say and do. Be with us, O Lord, for we cannot navigate through these times without you. Be with us, O Lord, for we yearn to be united in the mission of Jesus, helping the blind to see, the lame to walk and setting the oppressed free. This we ask in Jesus' name. Amen.

O Mary, conceived without sin, pray for us who have recourse to thee.

## Like a Motherless Child

Mother Church, I am here.
Mother Church, I am ready.
Mother Church, I am willing.

Mother Church, I have been knocking for years.
You have locked me out for years.
I will not go away.
I will not disappear.
You have to open your doors.
I will not stop knocking.

Mother Church,
I will knock until there is a hole in your door.
I will come in through the hole.
I will bring my open heart and my open mind.
I will bring my mother, my God.

Yes, Mother Church
I am here.
I am knocking.
I am willing.
I am ready.

I will no longer feel like a "Motherless Child."

## National Black Catholic Congress Prayer

O Lord our God,
under the shadow of your wings
we have found refuge, strength and hope.
We know that you are with us today,
just as you were present with those gone before us,
upon whose shoulders we now stand.
You were with our ancestors
as they journeyed to this land;
their strength they gained from you.
You were with past generations,
who sojourned through tough times and rough places;
their hope they gained from you.
Time and again with an outstretched arm
you delivered them as they clung to you;
their faith they gained from you.
Lord, we call upon you to do for us today
what you did for others in the past.
Lead us, your people,
Through this new place and time in history.
Bless this work of the National Black Catholic Congress.
Level the mountains of oppression we still face,
and make the crooked way straight.
Guide our feet to the places you want us to be,
and unite us in our struggle,
that we may be strengthened in our faith
and secure in your promise that
"the lame shall walk,
the blind shall see,
the oppressed shall be set free."
This we ask in the name of Jesus our Lord.
Amen.

## Prayer to Close a Meeting

Lord, we are leaving this meeting
Ready to take the challenge to make this a better group.

Thank you for your Loving Spirit,
Because we have some mountains to climb,
Some difficulties to overcome,
And some things that are in our way to move.

We know your power.
It is the power to work the impossible and we trust you.

We will keep our eyes on you.
We know this is where we will find our strength to keep
moving.

Dominion and power,
Lord you have and we ask
Your blessing as we say "Amen," and go forth from this place.

In the name of the Father, the Son and the Holy Spirit. Amen.

# PART FOUR

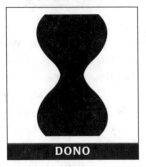

# "I'm Goin' To Sing"

## Prayers for Celebrations

*I'm goin' to sing when the spirit says sing.*
*I'm goin' to sing when the spirit says sing.*
*I'm goin' to sing when the spirit says sing.*
*And obey the spirit of the Lord.*[1]

**W**e have chosen "I'm Goin' To Sing" as the spiritual for this section of the book because of the energy, jubilation and thankfulness it produces in those who sing it because that is what these prayers are about—celebration and gratitude. When we face all manner of human-made and natural disasters, disappointments, disagreements, deaths and illnesses, it is sometimes difficult to see that in spite of all that we suffer in our lives, there is also so much we have cause to be thankful for every day. God wants us to experience the abundance of life and also wants to know we know that we are blessed. The movement of the Holy Spirit within each of us clears our vision so that we can recognize our blessings and it causes our hearts to pour out our thanks.

"I'm Goin' To Sing" testifies to the fact that all of the ways we express our joy and thanksgiving truly come from the movement of the Holy Spirit with us. This Holy Comforter and Divine Friend prompts us to sing, to dance, to shout and to clap to celebrate the blessings in our lives and to say thank you to our most gracious God for every fine gift we have and experience.

These prayers are for the wonderful times in our lives when we are gathered with family and friends to celebrate holidays, to feast and to revel in the gift of holiness in our presence. These prayers mark occasions such as the engagement of couples, jubilees and anniversaries, and holy days and feasts of the church.

We have chosen the *Dono*, the symbol of the drum, for these prayers of thanksgiving and celebration. In traditional African societies and in African American religious and secular culture, drums are used to call the community together in times of joy and celebration.

Cecilia A. Moore, PH.D.

## NOTE

[1] "I'm Goin' To Sing" in *American Negro Songs and Spirituals: A Comprehensive Collection of 230 Folk Songs, Religious and Secular, with a Foreword by John W. Work,* edited by John W. Work (New York: Bonanza Books, 1940), p. 226.

## Advent Season: Christmas Eve

"…without fear we might worship him in holiness and righteousness."
(Luke 1:74)

Christmas Eve. Anticipation. Children mentally count down the hours to morning to see what Santa left. For adults, it is the final day of shopping for gifts and finalizing preparations for the family dinner. All secular activities, of course. For Christians all over the world, this is a day to really prepare our hearts to commemorate the birth of Jesus Christ. We have meditated and reflected on the Word during the Advent journey, and our souls are now longing for the "Light of the World." We long for the One to bring hope to a hopeless world; to bring peace to a war-torn world; to bring light to those who still abide in darkness of the full knowledge of Jesus Christ. We are "the deer [who] longs for streams of water" (Psalm 42:1). We have heeded the wise counsel of the voice in the wilderness "to prepare the way of the LORD! Make straight in the wasteland a highway for our God!" (Isaiah 40:3). We pray, Lord, that we are ready.

O Most Holy God, we pause today to say that our hearts are ready to welcome the Baby Jesus; we are brimming over with joy that tomorrow we celebrate the birth of the Savior. Today, Lord, help us not to be distracted with the commercial fanfare and useless busyness; help us to focus on the glorious event that changed our lives forever. Help us, Father, to cherish and treasure the gift of your Son's birth, the beginning of our salvation history. Come, Baby Jesus, come into our hearts. In the name of your precious Son, we thank you, heavenly Father.

## The Work of Christmas

When the song of the
angels is stilled,
When the star in the sky is gone,
When the kings and princes
are home,
When the shepherds are
back with their flock,
The work of Christmas begins:
To find the lost,
To heal the broken,
To feed the hungry,
To release the prisoner,
To rebuild the nations,
To bring peace among brothers,
To make music in the heart.

## Kwanzaa Prayer

**Light black candle.**

*Umoja* is our prayer, Lord. We strive for unity at all times. In our churches, in our families. So Lord we pray for unity among African Americans and all peoples. We remember, Lord, these words of Holy Scripture.

*All:* Make every effort to preserve the unity, which has the Spirit as its origin and peace as its binding force. (Ephesians 4:3)

**Light red candle.**

*Kujichagulia* is our prayer, Lord. We pray for self-determination. Lord, we remember these words from Holy Scripture.

*All:* My children with humility, have self-determination and praise you as you deserve. (Sirach 10:27)

**Light green candle.**

*Ujima* is our prayer, Lord. We pray that we may build and maintain our community together and work collectively for the betterment of all people. We remember, Lord, these words from Holy Scripture.

*All:* The community of believers was of one heart and one mind. None of them claimed anything as their own, everything was held in common. (Acts 4:32)

**Light red candle.**

*Ujamaa* is our prayer, Lord. Economically supporting our communities is important to us, Lord. Help us to cooperate with one another, to share our wealth with our community and our church. We remember these words of Holy Scripture.

*All:* All believers continued to close fellowship and shared their belongings with one another. They would sell all their possessions and distribute the money among all, according to each one's needs. (Acts: 2:44-46)

**Light green candle.**

*Nia* is our prayer, Lord. We need purpose in this life to work together and struggle together. We remember these words from Holy Scripture.

*All*: His purpose was to rescue them from their enemies' hands and restore them to their father. (Genesis 37:22)

**Light red candle.**

*Kuumba* is our prayer, Lord. We need creativity, Lord, so that we can always do as much as we can to leave this community more beautiful and beneficial than when we inherited it. We remember these words from Holy Scripture.

*All:* There are different kinds of spiritual gifts but they all come from the same spirit. There are different ways to serve the same Lord, and we can each do different things. Yet the same God works in all of us and helps us in everything we do. (1 Corinthians 12:4-7)

**Light green candle.**

*Imani* is our prayer, Lord. We need to have faith. Faith in God, in ourselves and in our potential to be victorious in struggle. We need the faith of our forefathers and foremothers, who through hard work, struggle and a lot of love and understanding, gain victory for our people. We remember these words from Holy Scripture.

*All:* Have no fear of the sufferings to come. Remain faithful until death and I will give you the crown of life. (Revelation 2:10)

God of all, we lift up these prayers to you. Remember Lord, we want to walk with you in the garden of life. We ask all in the name of Jesus our Lord. Amen.

## Prayer in Honor of the Legacy of the Rev. Dr. Martin Luther King, Jr.

OPENING PRAYER

Gracious God, in every age you raise up women and men who give their lives for the message of your love.

Inspire us today with the memory of your servant, the Rev. Dr. Martin Luther King, Jr., a martyr for the gospel.

Let his faithfulness in following the cross be an example to us that we may bear full witness with our lives to your Son's victory over the slavery of sin and death, through Jesus, we pray. Amen.

CLOSING PRAYER

Good and Gracious God,
    May we leave this gathering today
committed to continue to fulfill the
    Dream of the Rev. Dr. Martin Luther King, Jr.,
by making your kingdom come on earth
    as it is in heaven and
by living together as loving sisters and brothers
    in Christ.
    In this we pray. Amen.

## Lenten Prayer

O, good and gracious God who reigns in heaven and in our hearts, I praise you and adore you. I know you as the giver of every good and perfect gift. I know you as my Creator, my Guide, my Protector.

I thank you for all that you have provided—my joys and moments of triumph; my family and loved ones; all that is yet to be. I thank you also for the sorrows, the pains, the disappointments and unfulfilled dreams. I know these things strengthen my faith in you and in myself. They teach me how to do things differently or to accept the decisions of those I love to find their own way, in their own time and in yours.

Forgive me Lord, for those times when I see things from my own perspective and not as you do. Forgive me when I am selfish and possessive and without enough trust in your mercy, providence and absolute love.

This day as I look toward the desert days of Lent, I need you once more and again as I prepare my mind, heart and soul to understand the unimaginable magnitude of your love for me.

When I *pray*, send your Spirit to pray for me. Hear my songs of love, praise, honor and worship. Hear my pleas for your intervention into the lives of those who need you most. And most of all, Lord, increase my faith. As I move through these forty days in the desert, I know you are there in front of me. Be by my side and at my back when I get weary, weak and lazy and want to go another way or even to turn around. Keep me strong to endure all that you have blessed me with.

When I *fast*, give me to know what it means to be without so that I will also know what it means to be filled with you only. May this fasting atone for those sins for which I failed to ask forgiveness.

When I *give* to others, remind me, dear Lord, that it is just a return for what you have given to me; to be thankful always; and even more generous. Help me to see the face of your Son in the least of us, even when it is difficult.

I know you hear and answer all prayer and so I place these forty days at your feet; thanking you, in Jesus' name, through his mother, Mary. Amen.

## Family Prayer at the Time of a Couple's Engagement

*Parent(s) of the engaged:* O my children, who we love so dearly, seek too the love that God extends to you this day. In the morning of your life, you enjoyed our love as parent(s) and as guide(s). Now in this afternoon hour of your life, bind the love we have given to you and create a new love of your own, a new family, a new home and a new nation. We give our blessings to you and this union as we remind you of the African proverbs that say, "A house built by God does not collapse," "And no one can uproot the tree which God has planted." So, together we pray for you and with you…

*All:* O Lord our God, our beloved are before you seeking your blessing, your love and your grace. We ask, O Lord, that you may look with great favor on *(name)* and *(name)*, for hope in you will not leave them disappointed. Fill their lives with joy and happiness and fend off situations that might harm their love and their family. Give them strength for the journey, wisdom to pass on to their children, courage to weather the storms and perseverance to hold onto in good times and in bad. Let them remember always that there are but three things that last: faith, hope and love, and the greatest of these is love. This we ask in Jesus' name. Amen.

## Wedding Toast

It is my honor and pleasure to lead this assembly in a toast to you, (*groom*) and (*bride*). It is a salutation to the love that has found you and the love you have found in each other. Even more, it is a toast to your standing in the face of the unknown to dare to profess an eternal love.

This requires hopefulness and reflects a belief in a goodness that runs through your veins. It is this hopefulness, this belief—this faith—if you will, that will help you to live the professed vows you have made today.

Remember that love is not something that happens to you, but rather something that you do. Remember that you control only the love you give, not the love you receive. Remember also that what you bring to your union is less important than what you do with what you bring—what you create, what you nurture, what you discover and what you hold sacred. Love doesn't lie dormant. It requires initiative and action.

Finally, understand that your love is not an entitlement ordained in the cosmos, but a gift of God from God. Honor God who manifests in your union daily with gratitude for this gift, and you will live happily all the days of your life.

Let us raise our glasses and offer a libation to your love:

May your marriage be a long and continuous journey of personal growth and adventure.

May you have friends to stand by you in good times and in bad times.

May you know and believe in the love that God has for us all, and that God is love and they who abide in love abide in God, and God in them. (1 John 4:16)

## Magnificat of a Golden Jubilarian

I call out with all my being,
"What a mighty God I serve;
What a loving God I serve!"

This mighty God has done great things for me
and through me.

Holy indeed is his name.

By his might and love, he has dispelled
fear from my heart and empowered
me to rise above my weaknesses
to glorify his name by loving service.

How can I repay my God for his goodness
to me?
I will proclaim his greatness to all who
will listen.
"What a mighty God I serve!
What a loving God I serve!"

Let everyone join me in
giving praise, honor and glory to
my mighty God.

Amen, Amen, Amen.

## Thanksgiving Prayer

This Thanksgiving let those of us who have much and those who have little gather at the welcoming table of the Lord. At this blessed feast, may rich and poor alike remember that we are called to serve one another and to walk together in God's gracious world. With thankful hearts we praise our God who like a loving parent denies us no good thing.

Today and every day, it pleases God for us to sit as brothers and sisters as we share the bounty of the earth and the grace God has placed in each blessed soul. For this we all give thanks and praise to our loving and gracious God.

# PART FIVE

**SANKOFA**

# "When the Saints Go Marching In"
## Prayers to the Saints and Ancestors

*Oh, when the saints go marching in,*
*Oh, when the saints go marching in,*
*Oh, Lord, I want to be in that number,*
*When the saints go marching in.*[1]

**W**ith great determination this spiritual declares the highest aspiration of every Christian. We all want "to be in that number" at the end of time when the saints of God gather around God's throne with all who have died in Christ and celebrate the victory of our salvation by God from all trials and tribulation. Though this spiritual reflects this fundamental Christian belief and desire, its roots are most strong in

West African traditional religions that formed the foundation of faith of enslaved African Americans who first raised its strains. It is about the ancestors.

Yoruba traditional religion teaches that all who live a good life, fulfill their destinies on earth, serve the gods and remember the ancestors have a life in heaven to look forward to. Therefore, the aim of each person is to live a worthy life so that they may live again in the company of the gods and the ancestors. The ancestors are all of those who after living a worthy life, died and returned to life in heaven. The connection between the living and the dead is indeed strong. The ancestors help to watch over the living, and they advocate on behalf of the living who seek their intercession with the gods. The ancestors are beloved, honored and respected by the living, and all of the living strive to become ancestors for becoming an ancestor is the only way to live on in heaven.

Though the Yoruba do not reject their lives on earth or disregard the merits and beauty of the earth and their earthly existence, they do see their lives on earth as temporary. How one lives this life on earth determines whether or not they will possess eternal life in heaven. In fact, a Yoruba proverb advises, "the world is a marketplace but heaven is home." However beautiful and lovely one's life here is or however sad and tragic one's life here is, it is not the final life. So live well now. There is so much more to look forward to in heaven, living with the deities and the ancestors.

These Yoruba beliefs and principles regarding the next life and the ancestors resonate very strongly with Roman Catholic teachings about the call of all people to live lives of holiness and with Catholic teaching regarding the lives of those who die in friendship with Christ. The church teaches us to strive to live lives of justice, compassion, peace, forgiveness and love and to look forward to the last day when all who have died in Christ will rejoice with God, the Father, Son and Holy Spirit, with the saints, and with all who have died in

Christ. This day will be a day of peace and justice and grand celebration that will never end.

Though many would hardly believe it, "When the Saints Go Marching In" is a song about death and about the triumph of life over death. "When the Saints Go Marching In" boldly declares the desire of its singers for a life-eternal with God and all those who have become saints, friends of God and their faith in God's promise of salvation and reunion.

The prayers in this section are for the dead, for those who grieve, for saints who hold special places of honor in the faith of African and African American Catholics, for the intercession of the saints, and for remembering and thanking all of the ancestors whose presence we miss on earth but who joyously and anxiously await reunion with us one day in heaven.

The *Sankofa* is our symbol for these prayers. This lovely backward-looking bird reminds us that we must never forget, that we must learn from our past and honor it, and that the greatest gift of love we can give our ancestors is to faithfully remember them.

Cecilia A. Moore, PH.D.

## NOTE

[1] Traditional.

## A Prayer-Poem in Honor of Our African Ancestors Who Perished in the Middle Passage

Although we do not remember the old tongues
Although we do not remember the old ways
You remember us.
Your blood is our blood; our blood is your blood.
May our lives hallow your deaths.

Although we do not remember the old tongues
Although we do not remember the old ways
You remember us.
Your blood is our blood; our blood is your blood.
May our lives be a living offering to honor your sacrifice.

Although we do not remember the old tongues
Although we do not remember the old ways
You remember us.
Your bones are our bones; our bones are your bones
May our freedom vindicate your bondage.

Before the Great Throne, lift up our cause; it is your cause.
Before the Great Throne, lift up our lives; we are your portion.
Before the Great Throne, lift up our tears; they are your tears.
Forever, you are ours, we are yours.

Although we do not remember the old tongues
Although we do not remember the old ways
We remember you.

Your voices ring in all our songs.
Your anguish cries out in all our sorrow.
Your suffering testifies in our struggle.
Your blood is our blood; our blood is your blood.

Although we do not remember the old tongues
Although we do not remember the old ways
We remember you.

## Prayer for the Beatification of Henriette Delille

O good and gracious God,
You called Henriette Delille
to give herself in service and in love
to the slaves and the sick,
to the orphan and the aged,
to the forgotten and the despised.

Grant that inspired by her life,
we might be renewed in heart and mind.
If it be your will,
may she one day be raised
to the honor of sainthood.
By her prayers,
may we live in harmony and peace.
Through Jesus Christ, our Lord.
Amen.

*If favors are received, please notify: Friends of Mother Henriette Delille, 6901 Chef Menteur Highway, New Orleans, LA 70126.*

## Magnificat

Every fiber of my being
what was, what is, what shall be,
magnifies my God
who magnified
Katharine Drexel and Josephine Bakhita.
My spirit towers
on eagle's wings
because my God's smile
blazes on earth and in heaven
and causes every living being to rejoice.

God's strength caught us up
and carried us to greatness
through the magnanimity of his
new saints.
His love transcended space and time
and now, all hasten to touch him.

Gracious God, you are a surge of justice.
You twist the paths of the proud.
The weight of the oppressor you lift.
The lowly whom you love
you elevate.
With your bare hands
you set the banquet table
and with your compassionate heart
you invite us all to eat your manna from heaven.

Our ancestors you have held and healed.
Ourselves you daily lead and guide.
Our future grows at this magnified moment of grace.
Because you, O God, in whom I exult
have shown infinite mercy.

## Prayer for Venerable Pierre Toussaint

Venerable Pierre Toussaint, you gave your life in service
to others.

Born into slavery, you spent forty-five years tending to the
needs and wishes of your master and mistress and your heart
did not grow hard or bitter.

You did not let your status as a slave blind you to your God-
given dignity or that of your brothers and sisters.

Once freed, you devoted yourself to the needy and poor you
saw all around you.

Instead of storing up the wealth your talents earned for you,
you used your wealth to care for orphans and to buy freedom
for your enslaved brothers and sisters.

Your generous heart knew no bounds.

Your fidelity to God was a witness for all to see.

Pierre, may your love for all of humanity, your faith in a loving
and generous God, your ability to see the dignity of all
people, and your perseverance in the face of oppression be
a source of encouragement and strength for us today. Amen.

## Prayer to Our Mother of Africa

Mary, Our Mother of Africa,
Hear the drumbeat of our prayers.
May your Son, Jesus, continue
To bring us joy, relieve our tensions,
And forgive us our sins.
Help us to walk in his Light.
Help us to help others do the same;
And bring us to life everlasting
With the holy saints and angels. Amen.

## Disquieting Silence

*This liturgical poem, "Qinie," is in Ge'ez, the liturgical language of Eritrean and Ethiopian Christianity.*

Halleluia—em me'Amuqe qelayat

we'imkeresse midre (Afriqiya) maHtsen

ge'Are emm weHitsanat ma'Edote baHir sdudan

tserHa habieke mel'Elte semayat aryam

lemint armemke hulqe mewa'El azman

Hawts Hizbeke werqe eton Huruyan

*Alleluia—From the deep seas*
*And from (Africa) earth's womb*
*Mother groaning for her children*
*Dispersed beyond far shores,*
*Cried out to you in the high heavens.*
*Disquieting silence for ages and centuries?*
*Come! Visit your people, purified,*
*By fire like precious gold.*

## Prayer to Saint Jude

O most holy apostle, Saint Jude, faithful servant and friend of Jesus, the church honors and invokes you universally, as the patron of hopeless cases, of things almost despaired of. Pray for me, I am so helpless and alone.

Make use, I implore you, of that particular privilege given to you, to bring visible and speedy help where help is almost despaired of. Come to my assistance in this great need that I may receive the consolation and help of heaven in all my necessities, tribulations, and sufferings, particularly *(state your request)* and that I may praise God with you and all the elect forever.

I promise, O blessed Saint Jude, to be ever mindful of this great favor, to always honor you as my special and powerful patron, and to gratefully encourage devotion to you.
Amen.

## The Claver Prayer

God, Our Heavenly Father, you have given us life through the death and resurrection of your beloved Son, Jesus Christ.

Jesus, our saving Lord, you came into the world darkened by man's sin and gave it light through your teachings.

Holy Spirit, the Breath of God within us, you guide and enlighten us and give us the strength of our convictions.

Saint Peter Claver, who became an example for us, you showed us the Lord God, the Light of Christ, and the strength of the Holy Spirit.

We pray now that all we say and do in your honor may be a continuation of your work here on earth.

Saint Peter Claver, pray for us.

## Litany of Mary

mother of God
born of God's breath
mother of Africa
sista of Dunbar
single parent
imparter of wisdom
knower and teller of all stories
madonna of m.l.k.
dwelling for God
unafraid of tradition
leader of ministers
teacher of faith
mother of the executed
blues singer
keeper of peace
director of children
bearer of ancestors
leader for justice
tender to dignity

...pray for us!

## Prayer for the Beatification of Mother Mary Lange

Almighty and eternal God, you granted Mother Mary Lange extraordinary trust in your providence. You endowed her with humility, courage, holiness and an extraordinary sense of service to the poor and sick. You enabled her to found the Oblate Sisters of Providence and provide educational, social and spiritual ministry especially to the African American community. Mother Lange's love for all enabled her to see Christ in each person, and the pain of prejudice and racial hatred never blurred that vision.

Deign to raise her to the highest honors of the altar in order that, through her intercession, more souls may come to a deeper understanding and more fervent love of you.

Heavenly Father, glorify your heart by granting also this favor *(here mention your request)* which we ask through the intercession of your faithful servant, Mother Mary Lange. Amen.

*If favors are received, please notify: Lange Guild, 701 Gun Road, Baltimore, MD 21227.*

## Prayer to Saint Martin de Porres

To you Saint Martin de Porres we prayerfully lift up our hearts filled with serene confidence and devotion. Mindful of your unbounded and helpful charity to all levels of society and also of your meekness and humility of heart, we offer our petitions to you. Pour out upon our families the precious gifts of your solicitous and generous intercession; show to the people of every race and every color the paths of unity and of justice; implore from our Father in heaven the coming of his kingdom, so that through mutual benevolence in God men may increase the fruits of grace and merit the rewards of eternal life. Amen.

## Prayer in Honor of Saint Josephine Bakhita

Father,
you, who in your great mercy,
have freed Saint Josephine Bakhita
from slavery
to lead her to the dignity
of being your Daughter
and spouse of Christ,
grant us the grace to imitate her
in her great love for Jesus Crucified
and in the practice of charity,
and forgiveness.
Through Christ our Lord. Amen.

## PART SIX

**NYAME DUA**

# "Lord, I Want to Be a Christian"
## Traditional Catholic Prayers

*Lord, I want to be a Christian in-a my heart, in my heart,*
*Lord, I want to be a Christian in-a my heart, in my heart.*
*In my heart, in-a my heart,*
*Lord, I want to be a Christian in-a my heart, in-a my heart.*[1]

Through every prayer that we whisper alone, that we say with our families and friends, or that we proclaim when gathered for the celebration of the Eucharist, we express our sincere wishes to live as true followers of Christ and children of God. We share this desire for an increase in faith with every generation of Christians that has preceded us. And, we are heirs of a rich and beautiful legacy of prayers that our Christian ancestors of every age and culture have bequeathed to the future generations.

In this final section of *Songs of Our Hearts, Meditations of Our Souls*, we offer some of the most commonly used and most beloved prayers of the Catholic tradition. We use these prayers to praise and give thanks to the Lord, to ask for those things we need and desire, and to express our desire for an increase of faith so that we might love and care for each other as Jesus does for each of us.

The spiritual we have selected, "Lord, I Want to Be a Christian In-a My Heart," is a simple yet profound meditation on the most deeply felt wish of each person who has answered the call to follow Jesus. We want to be more than Christian in name. We want to be Christian in our hearts because it is Christ alive in our hearts that makes it possible for us to live as he lived, to believe as he believed and to love as he loved. The spiritual also expresses the desire to be more loving, to be more holy and to be like Jesus in our hearts. None of these things is easy to do, but all are impossible without our prayers and acceptance of God's grace. Here we turn to the prayers of the church that have been a source of blessing for Catholic Christians of every age and culture and that continue to be a blessing to us, too.

The *Nyame Dua* symbolizes God's presence and protection. In Ghana it is often used to mark a place where religious rituals are performed. It is also commonly used in the fronts of houses. Vessels shaped in the form of the *Nyame Dua* are used to hold water and herbs used in purification rituals and blessing rituals. The *Nyame Dua* also carries with it the meaning of the altar, the place where sacrifices are made to God. We have chosen this symbol for "Lord, I Want to Be a Christian" because we want to join the centuries of Christians who have used these prayers to enter into God's presence, to feel the blessings of God and to prepare their hearts and minds to serve as altars of God.

Cecilia A. Moore, PH.D.


## NOTE

[1] "Lord, I Want to Be a Christian In-a My Heart," in *The Book of American Negro Spirituals including the Book of American Negro Spirituals and the Second Book of Negro Spirituals,* edited by James Wheldon Johnson and J. Rosamond Johnson (New York: The Viking Press, 1969), pp. 72-73.

## Sign of the Cross

In the name of the Father, and of the Son, and of the Holy Spirit. Amen.

## Lord's Prayer

Our Father, who art in heaven, hallowed be your name; your Kingdom come; your will be done, on earth as it is in heaven. Give us this day our daily bread; and forgive us our trespasses as we forgive those who trespass against us; and lead us not into temptation, but deliver us from evil. Amen.

## Hail Mary

Hail Mary, full of grace! the Lord is with you; blessed are you among women, and blessed is the fruit of your womb, Jesus. Holy Mary, Mother of God, pray for us sinners, now and at the hour of our death. Amen.

## Glory Be

Glory be to the Father, and to the Son, and to the Holy Spirit. As it was in the beginning, is now, and ever shall be, world without end. Amen.

## Apostles' Creed

I believe in God, the Father Almighty,
   creator of heaven and earth.

I believe in Jesus Christ, his only Son, our Lord.
   He was conceived by the power of the Holy Spirit
      and born of the Virgin Mary.
   He suffered under Pontius Pilate,
      was crucified, died, and was buried.
   He descended to the dead.
   On the third day he arose again.
   He ascended into heaven,
      and is seated at the right hand of the Father.
He will come again to judge the living and the dead.

I believe in the Holy Spirit,
   the holy Catholic church,
   the communion of saints,
   the forgiveness of sins,
   the resurrection of the body,
   and the life everlasting. Amen.

## The Nicene Creed

We believe in one God,
the Father, the almighty,
maker of heaven and earth,
of all that is, seen and unseen.

We believe in one Lord, Jesus Christ,
the only Son of God,
eternally begotten of the Father,
God from God, Light from Light,
true God from true God,
begotten, not made, one in Being with the Father.
Through him all things were made.
For us men and for our salvation
he came down from heaven:

by the power of the Holy Spirit
he was born of the Virgin Mary, and became man.

For our sake he was crucified under Pontius Pilate;
he suffered, died, and was buried.
On the third day he rose again
in fulfillment of the Scriptures;
he ascended into heaven
and is seated at the right hand of the Father.
He will come again in glory to judge the living and the dead,
and his kingdom will have no end.

We believe in the Holy Spirit, the Lord, the giver of life,
who proceeds from the Father and the Son.
With the Father and the Son he is worshiped and glorified.
He has spoken through the Prophets.

We believe in one holy catholic and apostolic Church.
We acknowledge one baptism for the forgiveness of sins.
We look for the resurrection of the dead,
    and the life of the world to come. Amen.


## The Angelus

V. The Angel spoke God's message to Mary
R. and she conceived of the Holy Spirit
V. Hail Mary,…
R. Holy Mary,…


V. I am the lowly servant of the Lord
R. Let it be done to me according to your word.
V. Hail Mary,…
R. Holy Mary,…


V. And the Word became flesh
R. and lived among us.
V. Hail Mary,…
R. Holy Mary,…
V. Pray for us, Holy Mother of God,
R. That we may become worthy of the promises of Christ

Let us pray
Lord, fill our hearts with your grace: once, through the message
of an angel you revealed to us the incarnation of your Son;
now, through his suffering and death lead us to the glory of
his resurrection.

We ask this through Christ our Lord.

## The Mysteries of the Rosary

*(With recommended Scripture meditations)*

### The Joyful Mysteries *(Saturday and Monday)*

1. The annunciation of the archangel Gabriel to the Virgin Mary *(Luke 1:26-38)*
2. The visitation of the Virgin Mary to the parents of Saint John the Baptist *(Luke 1:39-45)*
3. The birth of our Lord at Bethlehem *(Luke 2:1-20)*
4. The presentation of our Lord in the Temple *(Luke 2:22-35)*
5. The finding of our Lord in the Temple *(Luke 2:41-52)*

### The Mysteries of Light, or Luminous Mysteries *(Thursday)*

1. The baptism of our Lord in the Jordan *(Matthew 3:13-17)*
2. The self-manifestation of our Lord at the wedding at Cana *(John 2:1-12)*
3. The proclamation of the Kingdom of God by our Lord, with his call to conversion *(Mark 1:15)*
4. The transfiguration of our Lord *(Matthew 17:1-9)*
5. The institution of the Eucharist by our Lord, as the sacramental expression of the Paschal Mystery *(Matthew 26:26-28)*

### The Sorrowful Mysteries *(Tuesday and Friday)*

1. The agony of our Lord in the Garden of Gethsemane *(Matthew 26:46; Mark 14:26-42; Luke 22:39-53; John 18:1-12)*
2. The scourging of our Lord at the pillar *(Matthew 27:15-26; Mark 15:1-15)*
3. The crowning of our Lord with thorns *(Matthew 16:24-28, 27:27-31; Mark 15:16-19; Luke 23:6-11; John 19:1-7)*
4. The carrying of the cross by our Lord to Calvary *(Mark 8:31-38; Matthew 16:20-25; Luke 23:26-32; John 19:17-22)*
5. The crucifixion and death of our Lord *(Mark 15:33-39; Luke 23:33-46; John 19:23-37; Acts 22:22-24)*

**The Glorious Mysteries** *(Wednesday and Sunday)*

1. The resurrection of our Lord from the dead *(Matthew 28:1-10; Mark 16:1-18; Luke 24:1-12; John 20: 1-10)*
2. The ascension of our Lord into heaven *(Matthew 28:16-20; Luke 24:44-53; Acts 1:1-11)*
3. The descent of the Holy Spirit upon the apostles *(Acts 2:1-11)*
4. The assumption of our Blessed Lady into heaven *(Revelation 21:1-6)*
5. The coronation of our Blessed Lady as Queen of Heaven and Earth *(Revelation 7:1-4, 9-12, 21:1-6)*

## Hail, Holy Queen

Hail, holy Queen, Mother of mercy! Hail our life, comfort and hope! To you do we cry, poor banished children of Eve. To you do we send up our sighs, mourning and weeping in this vale of tears. Turn then, most gracious advocate, your eyes of mercy toward us; and after this, our exile, show unto us the blessed fruit of your womb Jesus. O clement, O loving, O sweet Virgin Mary! Amen.

Pray for us, O holy Mother of God, that we may be made worthy of the promises of Christ.

## Memorare

Remember, most gracious Virgin Mary, that never was it known that anyone who fled to your protection, implored your help, or sought your intercession was left unaided. Inspired with this confidence, I fly to you, O Virgin of virgins, my mother. To you I come; before you I stand, sinful and sorrowful. O Mother of the Word Incarnate, despise not my petitions, but in your mercy, hear and answer me. Amen.

## Saint Augustine Prayer

Breathe in me, O Holy Spirit
That my thoughts may all be holy;
Act in me, O Holy Spirit,
That my work, too, may be holy;
Draw my heart, O Holy Spirit,
That I love but what is holy;
Strengthen me, O Holy Spirit,
To defend all that is Holy;
Guard me, then, O Holy Spirit,
That I always may be holy.

## *Anima Christi*, or Soul of Christ

Soul of Christ, sanctify me.
Body of Christ, save me.
Blood of Christ, inebriate me.
Water from the side of Christ, wash me.
Passion of Christ, strengthen me.
O good Jesus, hear me.
Within your wounds, hide me.
Separate from you, let me never be.
From the malignant enemy, defend me.
At the hour of death, call me.
To come to you, bid me,
That I may praise you in the company

Of your saints, for all eternity.  Amen.

## Peace Prayer of Saint Francis

*(attributed to Saint Francis)*

Lord, make me an instrument of your peace;
where there is hatred, let me sow love;
where there is injury, pardon;
where there is doubt, faith;
where there is despair, hope;
where there is darkness, light;
and where there is sadness, joy.

O, Divine Master,
grant that I may not so much seek
to be consoled as to console;
to be understood as to understand;
to be loved as to love;
for it is in giving that we receive;
it is in pardoning that we are pardoned;
and it is in dying
that we are born to eternal life.

## Stations of the Cross

First Station: Jesus Is Condemned to Death
Second Station: Jesus Accepts His Cross
Third Station: Jesus Falls the First Time
Fourth Station: Jesus Meets His Sorrowful Mother
Fifth Station: Simon Helps Jesus Carry the Cross
Sixth Station: Veronica Presents Her Veil to Jesus
Seventh Station: Jesus Falls the Second Time
Eighth Stations: Jesus Speaks to the Weeping Women
Ninth Station: Jesus Falls the Third Time
Tenth Station: Jesus Is Stripped of His Garments
Eleventh Station: Jesus Is Nailed to the Cross
Twelfth Station: Jesus Dies on the Cross
Thirteenth Station: Jesus Is Taken Down From the Cross
Fourteenth Station: Jesus Is Laid Into the Tomb

## Act of Contrition

O my God, I am heartily sorry for having offended you, and
I detest all my sins, known and unknown, not only because
I dread the loss of heaven and dread the pains of hell, and
not only because you are my Creator, my Redeemer and my
Sanctifier, but most of all because my sins have offended you,
my God, who are all good in yourself and deserving of all my
love. I firmly resolve, with the help of your grace, to confess
my sins, to do penance and to amend my life. Amen.

## Jesus Prayer

Lord Jesus Christ,
Son of the living God,
Have mercy on me, a sinner.

# Acknowledgments and Contributors

The editors would like to thank the many men and women and organizations who so willingly contributed prayers to *Songs of Our Hearts, Meditations of Our Souls.* The prayer book is richer for these contributions.

**Part One: "I Know There's A God Somewhere"**

"Sweet Holy Spirit" by Donna Grant-Lane
"Morning Prayer" by Michael E. Russell, a Knight of Peter Claver
"No Certain Time, No Certain Place to Praise the Lord and See His Face" by Anthony Irvin
"Evening Prayer" by Michael E. Russell, A Knight of Peter Claver
"Self-Sacrifice" by Aliya Matthews-Ait
"Prayer for Black Catholic Men" by Herb Grimes

"Words and Wisdom" by Michael E. Russell, a Knight of Peter Claver

"Alphabet Prayer" by Elencie Shynes

"Footprints" in Public Domain

"Butterfly" by Timone Newsome

"Paradise" by Aliya Matthews-Ait

"He IS" by Aliya Matthews-Ait

"The Path" by Aliya Matthews-Ait

### Part Two: "This Little Light of Mine"

"Prayer for African American Families" by Fr. Jim Goode, O.F.M.

"Prayer for African American Families" by Therese Wilson Favors

"Prayer for African American Families…in the Times of Trouble" by Therese Wilson Favors

"Family Reunion Prayer" by Madelaine C. Gentry

"A Father's Prayer" by Lester Smith

"Prayer of a Mother" by Opal Easter

"A Scripture to Inspire You as You Teach" by Therese Wilson Favors

"Angel Prayer" by Donna Grant-Lane

"A Prayer for Catechists and Youth Ministers as You Teach" by Therese Wilson Favors

"Prayer for Students" by Ansel Augustine

"Morning Prayer of Thanks" by Diana Allen

"Parents' Baptism Prayer" by Cecilia A. Moore

"Prayer for the Blessing of Youth Councils" by Ansel Augustine

"Prayer for Those Who Work With Young People" by Harrison Havard, Jr.

"First Communion Prayer" by Cecilia A. Moore

"Franciscan Mealtime Blessing" from Br. Arlen Harris, O.F.M. CAP.

**Part Three: "Wade in the Water"**

"Call to Prayer" by Fr. Tom L. Jackson, O.P.

"Hurricane Katrina Prayer of Consolation" by Fr. Jim Goode, O.F.M.

"Flood Waters" by Sr. M. Roland Lagarde, S.B.S.

"Prayer to the Gentle Healer" by Vivian Rouson

"Prayer of Petition" by Elencie Shynes

"Prayer for Deliverance" by Brigette Maria Rouson

"Prayer for Those Suffering From HIV/AIDS" used with permission of the United States Catholic Bishops

"I'm Going Through" by Yvonne S. Finley

"Prayer for the National Gathering of Black Catholic Women" by Sr. M. Roland Lagarde, S.B.S.

"Addict's Prayer" by Barbara R. Minnick

"A Prayer for Reconciliation" by Angela Redmond

"Vocation Prayer" by Jesse Cox, O.P., and Mary Therese Johnson, O.P.

"Prayer for Vocations" by Sr. Beatrice Jeffries, S.B.S., used with permission of the National Coalition for Church Vocations

"Prayer for the Lost and Confused" by Timone Newsome

"Prayer for Proper Use of Talents" by Harrison Havard, Jr.

"Prayer for Those Seeking God" by Timone Newsome

"A Prayer for Social Justice" by Fr. Patrick Smith

"Prayer for Guidance" by Timone Newsome

"Prayer for Those Who Are Suffering" by Timone Newsome

"Prayer Haiku" by Lizette Rouson-Benefield

"An African Prayer" contributed by Richard Cheri

"Prayer for Choirs, Choir Directors, Ministers of Music and Musicians" by Sheila Adams

"Prayer for Solidarity and Steadfastness in Ministry" by Therese Wilson Favors

"Prayer for Discernment for Black Catholic Leaders" by C. Vanessa White

"Fear Not" by Carolyn Darensbourg

"Prayer for Unity in Evangelization Ministry" by Therese Wilson Favors

"Like a Motherless Child" by Mary Norfleet Johnson

"National Black Catholic Congress Prayer" used with permission of the National Black Catholic Congress

"Prayer to Close a Meeting" by Marcella Herndon

## Part Four: "I'm Goin' To Sing"

"Advent Season: Christmas Eve" by Burma Hill

"The Work of Christmas" from *The Mood of Christmas*, by Howard Thurman, used with the permission of Friends United Press

"Kwanzaa Prayer" adapted by Sr. Jamie T. Phelps, O.P.

"Prayer in Honor of the Legacy of Rev. Dr. Martin L. King, Jr." by C. Vanessa White

"Lenten Prayer" by Claudine Pannell-Goodlett

"Family Prayer at the Time of a Couple's Engagement" by Therese Wilson Favors

"Wedding Toast" by Andrew Lyke, S.F.O.

"Magnificat of a Golden Jubilarian" by Sr. Loretta Theresa Richards, F.H.M.

"Thanksgiving Prayer" by Cecilia A. Moore

## Part Five: "When the Saints Go Marching In"

"A Prayer-Poem in Honor of Our African Ancestors Who Perished in the Middle Passage" by M. Shawn Copeland

"Prayer for the Beatification of Henriette Delille" used with the permission of the Sisters of the Holy Family

"Magnificat" by Sr. M. Roland Lagarde, S.B.S.

"Prayer for Venerable Pierre Toussaint" by Cecilia A. Moore

"Prayer to Our Mother of Africa" by Jacqueline E. Wilson

"Disquieting Silence" by Fessahaye Mebrahtu

"Prayer to Saint Jude" used with permission of the Sons of the Immaculate Heart of Mary

"The Claver Prayer" used with permission of the Knights of Peter Claver, Inc., and the Knights of Peter Claver Ladies Auxiliary

"Litany of Mary" by Dean Blietz

"Prayer for the Beatification of Mother Mary Lange" used with the permission of the Oblate Sisters of Providence

"Prayer to Saint Martin de Porres" from www.Catholic.org

"Prayer in Honor of Saint Josephine Bakhita" used with the permission of the Canossian Daughters of Charity

**Part Six: "Lord, I Want to Be a Christian"**

Saint Augustine Prayer, from www.Catholic.org.